A Little Hands Early Learning Book

SHAPES, SIZES & MORE SURPRISES!

Mary Tomczyk

illustrations by Loretta Trezzo Braren

WILLIAMSON PUBLISHING • CHARLOTTE, VERMONT

Little Hands and *Kids Can!* are registered trademarks of Williamson Publishing Company.

Library of Congress Cataloging-in-Publication Data

Tomczyk, Mary, 1954-
    Shapes, sizes & more surprises!: a little hands early learning book/Mary Tomczyk.
    p. cm. —(A Williamson little hands book;2)
    Includes index.
    Summary: Over sixty learning experiences explore shapes, numbers, and counting.
    ISBN 0-913589-95-0 (alk. paper)
    1. Geometry—Juvenile literature. [1. Geometry.] I. Title.
    II. Series.
    QA445.5.T66 1995
    619'.5—dc20

Cover design: Trezzo–Braren Studio
Interior design: Trezzo–Braren Studio
Illustrations: Loretta Trezzo Braren
Printing: Capital City Press

Williamson Publishing Co.
P.O. Box 185
Charlotte, Vermont 05445
1-800-234-8791

Manufactured in the United States of America

10 9 8 7 6 5 4 3 2 1

Dedication

To my children, Dawn, David, Jim, and Kim,
who brought these ideas to life.

To my husband, Fred, who has been my partner
and greatest encourager — without him, this book
would never have been written.

Contents

Foreword ● 5

To the Children
Tips for Grown-Ups

Shaping Up! ■ 7

Shape Art
My Book of Shapes
Pudding Paint Designs
Place Mat Patterns
Sponge Paint Shapes
Travel Hunt
Shape Detective
Plenty of Patterns

Lots Of Colors ▲ 23

Tissue Paper Rainbow
Shaving Cream Pictures
Coffee Can Color Sort
Color Walk
Racing Colors
Ice Painting

Amazing Alphabet ● 35

ABC Cookies
Trace-A-Letter
Bean Fun
Body Letters
Palm Drawings
Make-A-Match

Count Me In! ■ 49

Egg Carton Count
Face Fun
Count-and-Eat Jewelry
Jumping Numbers
Number Puzzles
Paper Chain Counting Calendar
Creative Creatures
A Counting Pictograph

Sort It Out! ▲ 67

Big and Small
Food Sort
Imagination Station
Animal Round-Up
Memories Box
Dough Bead Necklace
Matching Groups

Let's Compare! ● 81

What's That Sound?
Mirror Pals
Big and Little Day
In the Bag
What's Missing?
Self-Portraits
I'm Thinking of Something
Finger Food Fun
Dice Designs
Touch Will Tell
Three-Sense Challenge

I Understand! ■ 103

Animals In Our House!
Rhymes and Finger Plays
I Like. . .
Tricky Tales
Noise Makers
Five-Finger Hunt
Happy-Sad Masks
Recycled Greeting Cards

Movin' & Shakin' ▲ 119

Paper Burst
Paint With Water
Obstacle Course
Bounce and Count
Build-A-Person
Cutting Up!
Opposites Attract
Yes, I Can!
Two Hands — Or One!

Index to Early Learning Skills ● 138

Acknowledgements

I would like to thank my friends Jeanine Hughes and Ruth Gauci for lending their expertise, Mark and John Gabriele for their thoughtfulness, Edwarda Tomczyk, Bob Gabriele, Josephine Del Papa, and Mary and Tony Gabriele, for their understanding, encouragement, and support.

To the Children

Wouldn't it be fun to go on an exciting adventure with lots of surprises? That's what learning is — an exciting adventure that never ends! Along the way, you'll discover things you know, and things you don't. And if you make some mistakes along the way, that's good: that's part of learning, too. Best of all, when you learn something new, it's like finding a little treasure: you can keep what you've learned forever!

This book is full of fun things for you to do. There are counting games, art projects, alphabet activities, things to sort and compare, color walks, stories to tell, water play, and even painting with pudding.

Most of the activities you can do by yourself, some will require a grown-up partner, and some are games to play with a friend. Remember always to ask for help if you need it: that's one way we learn!

And, don't forget: safety first!

Lots of wonderful experiences are waiting for you in the pages of this book. Are you ready to begin the adventure?

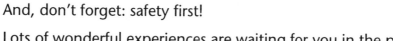
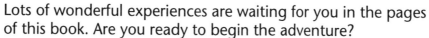

Tips For Grown-Ups

Discovering the world through a young child's eyes is one of the greatest pleasures any of us can know. This book is a collection of activities and games that are designed to smooth your way along that path of discovery, while you help each child develop basic learning skills for future personal growth.

Young children have an almost insatiable desire to explore the world around them — and I hope that these activities can help that desire to blossom and grow into a habit they will enjoy throughout their lives.

All of us learn best by doing and that may be even more the case for our youngest learners. That's why this book is filled with lots of hands-on, interactive experiences designed to be done together: some require more of your input, some less. Be wary, of course, of children putting objects in their mouths and decide when tools like a stapler, safety scissors, or a hole punch can be used safely. Young children should always be supervised.

Since children at this age vary so widely in their abilities, experiences, and interests, I have given wide age ranges for each activity and these are only to be used as the roughest guidelines. Each section is organized from simplest to more complex activities, but you needn't do them in order. If an activity doesn't spark interest or seems too difficult, try something different, and go back to it again at another time. For any given activity, there are several additional ideas for things to do; these can be used to reinforce and broaden the learning and give children another approach to a particular skill.

The activities are grouped into basic early learning skills — those skills which form the basis for future adventures in learning. There is also an index on pages 138–139 cross-referencing different skill-building activities to help you select activities to share for fun and growth.

As I mentioned in To the Children, learning is an adventure — you are the guide! Be enthusiastic, laugh often, listen carefully, respond thoughtfully, and enjoy this journey together.

Mary Tomczyk

Shaping Up!

A ball, a box, a straw...everything has its own special shape — even you! The shape of each thing helps us to know what it is. Let's have some fun with different shapes!

Shape Art

 AGES 2-6

Which shape is your favorite: a circle, a square, or a triangle? Make your favorite shape into a piece of Shape Art to hang in your room.

HERE'S WHAT YOU NEED

- **Cardboard from cereal box**
- **Safety scissors**
- **Decorative items: uncooked macaroni, fabric scraps, buttons, gift wrap scraps, dried beans**
- **Glue**
- **String**

HERE'S WHAT YOU DO

1. Cut out your favorite shape from cardboard.

2. Spread the glue evenly over the cardboard shape. Press the decorative items into the glue, placing them very close together so the cardboard is covered completely. Let dry.

3. To hang, push string through a hole at the top of the shape, tie, and hang where you wish.

HEY! TRY A SQUARE OR TRIANGLE SHAPE

ALIKE AND DIFFERENT

Close your eyes and gently run your fingers over the shape you just made. Can you tell what the big shape is with your eyes closed? Can you feel the difference between the **hard** macaroni and the **soft** pieces of fabric?

MORE SURPRISES!

★ Make a frame for your favorite artwork by cutting out a large shape from the center of a piece of cardboard. Decorate the outer edges of your picture frame with colored squares, circles, and triangles cut from construction paper or shiny pieces of gift wrap. Tape a picture to the back and hang.

Silly Sayings

Have you heard grown-ups talk about "getting into shape"? They don't really mean getting into the shape of a triangle, of course. That would be funny. Getting into shape really means having a healthy body.

HELPING • HANDS

Focus on a particular shape for a day or a week. Celebrate Circle Day by baking muffins in round tins, eating lunch in a circle, or taking a walk to find five circular objects.

My Book of Shapes

AGES 2-6

How would you like to write and draw your own book? That's what you're going to be doing when you make your own Book of Shapes.

HERE'S WHAT YOU NEED

- Construction paper
- Old magazines
- Safety scissors
- Glue and crayons
- Textured materials (uncooked macaroni, sandpaper, fabric scraps)
- Paper punch and yarn

HERE'S WHAT YOU DO

1 Make your book about your favorite shape — circle, square, triangle, or rectangle.

2 Cut out pictures with your special shape in them from some old magazines.

3 Glue the cutout shapes onto several sheets of construction paper.

4 Make a cover for your Book of Shapes by drawing a big picture of your special shape on a sheet of construction paper. On top of the shape, you can glue macaroni, sandpaper, or fabric so it will be fun to touch.

5 Punch two holes through the left side of each page. Tie the pages together with yarn to make your book. Show your special shape book to your friends.

SILLY SAYINGS

You can't put a square peg into a round hole.

Why can't you put a square peg into a round hole? Because a square has four sides and four corners and a round hole (a circle) has no corners, so it wouldn't fit. But this saying can mean many other things, too. It can mean that things that are very different sometimes don't fit together in the usual manner.

HELPING • HANDS

Remember to gear this activity to each youngster's attention span. Keep your time together exciting, even if you find you have to keep it fairly short.

MORE SURPRISES!

★ Now that you know how to make a Book of Shapes, you can choose another shape to make into a book. How many shape books would you like to have?

★ As you read your Book of Shapes, it's fun to trace over each shape with your fingers.

★ People who can't see read books with their fingers. They use a special alphabet of letters made up of raised dots called *Braille* that they can recognize with their fingers. If you close your eyes and touch the shape on the cover of your book, can you "see" the shape through your fingertips?

Pudding Paint Designs

If painting with pudding sounds like a silly and sloppy thing to do, well, that's because it is! Best of all, you can lick your fingers when you're done!

AGES 2-6

HERE'S WHAT YOU NEED

1 package instant pudding mix, prepared according to directions

Butcher paper or finger-paint paper

Pencil

Newspaper

HERE'S WHAT YOU DO

1 Cover the table with newspaper. Cut off a big piece of paper.

2 While you wait for the pudding to thicken, ask a grown-up to help you draw some big shapes on the paper. Maybe you'll have a small circle come smashing into the side of a triangle!

3 Spoon some pudding onto the paper. Use your fingers to spread the pudding into your own personal masterpiece of shapes. Since you only have one color to work with, use your fingers, the palm of your hand, or make a fist to get different effects. Try pressing hard or sweeping lightly over the paint.

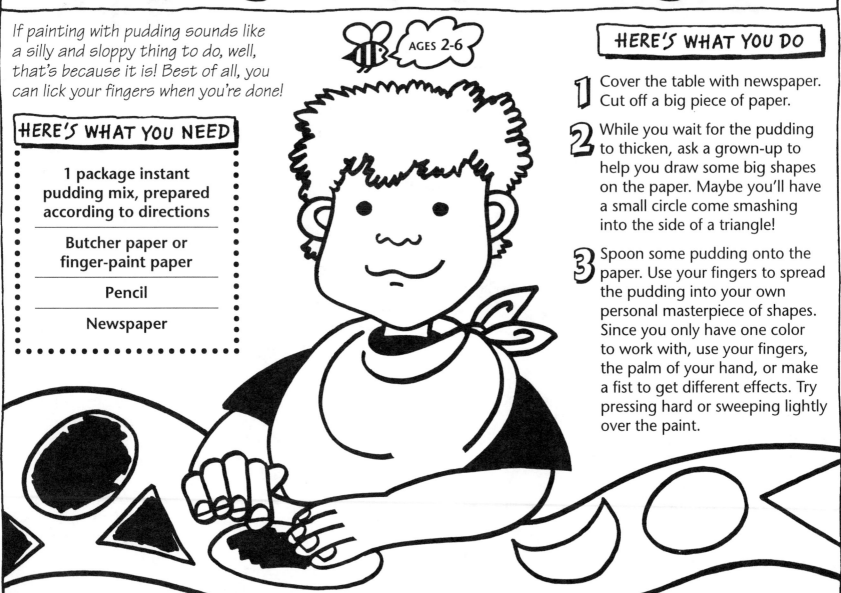

ALIKE AND DIFFERENT

Have you ever used finger paints? These are almost like pudding paints except, of course, you can't eat them. How else are pudding paints and finger paints different? How are they the same, or alike?

HELPING·HANDS

Some children will be more interested in creative drawing than in drawing shapes or letters. And, some children will not want to put their fingers into the pudding. Start with a little pudding. Talk about the **texture** of the paper and the **feeling** of the smooth pudding.

MORE SURPRISES!

★ Write your initials (the first letter of your first and last names) very large in pencil on your paper. See what kind of object, design, or even picture you can make out of each letter. If your name begins with an S, you might turn the S into a swan. If your name begins with a P, you might turn the P into a flower.

★ Many of the world's most famous artists learned to paint by experimenting first. They practiced painting with different shapes to discover what looked just right. Try using many shapes such as circles, squares, and triangles when you draw. What shapes do you like painting most?

★ Use your bare feet to paint a picture. Try painting a few numbers or spell your name with your toes! This can get pretty messy, though, so do it when you can paint outdoors, and keep a bucket of water and a towel handy.

★ Close your eyes and imagine a shape. Now, with your eyes still shut, use your fingers to paint what you are imagining.

Place Mat Patterns

AGES 3-6

Any series that repeats is called a pattern. Patterns are all around you in shapes, numbers, letters, colors, and designs. Can you figure out what comes next in this pattern? "Red-yellow-blue, red-yellow-blue, red-yellow-..." See, patterns are fun!

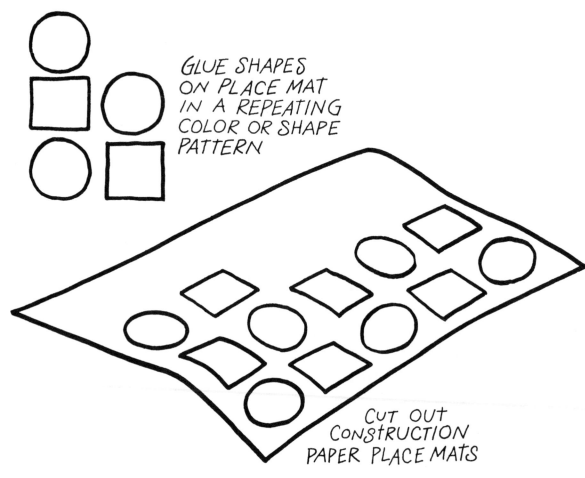

GLUE SHAPES ON PLACE MAT IN A REPEATING COLOR OR SHAPE PATTERN

CUT OUT CONSTRUCTION PAPER PLACE MATS

HERE'S WHAT YOU DO

1 Using cardboard templates of a circle, a square, and a triangle, trace and cut out several of each shape from different colors of paper.

2 Choose any two shapes to make a simple pattern such as circle-square, circle-square.

3 Choose a fourth color of construction paper for your place mat. Design a pattern of shapes and colors that you like and glue in place.

Patterns provide the foundation for making sense out of our surroundings and for understanding many subjects, from math to English. Encourage children to create patterns of their own such as a three-shape pattern, a color pattern, or even a pattern that uses both shapes and colors.

MORE SURPRISES!

★ Make place mats for each family member and talk about why you chose certain colors and shapes for each one.

★ Do you notice any other patterns at the dinner table? What about the knife, fork, and spoon?

★ Take turns around the dinner table pointing out patterns in the room.

Sponge Paint Shapes

 AGES 3-6

Enjoy creating your own Sponge Paint Shape design and decorate a t-shirt with shapes galore!

HERE'S WHAT YOU NEED

T-shirt

Sponge

Fabric paint

Contact paper

Safety scissors

Newspaper

HELPING · HANDS

As you guide each child through this activity, talk about shapes and colors and creative combinations. For a pattern, there needs to be a plan.

1. Cover a table with newspaper. Cut the sponge into pieces about the size of the palm of your hand.

2. Next, cut the contact paper in the shape of a large square — about the same size as your t-shirt.

3. Think about a simple design or pattern made up of shapes like circles, squares, triangles. Draw the design onto the back of the contact paper (you can trace around templates a grown-up helps you with). Cut the shapes out of the contact paper to make a stencil.

4. Peel the backing off your stencilled contact paper, and stick it to your special shirt. Dip your sponge lightly into the paint and dab it over all the uncovered areas. (It's okay if the paint goes onto the contact paper).

5. Let the shirt dry completely before removing the contact paper. Now you can wear your shape shirt and show your friends and family!

STICK CONTACT PAPER ON SHIRT FRONT

DIP SPONGE INTO PAINT AND DAB OVER CUT-OUT SHAPES IN STENCIL

Clean-Up Helpers

True sponges were animals that lived at the bottom of the ocean. The skeletons of these sponges make good cleaning tools because they're soft and they absorb a lot of water. The sponges you use to paint with, however, are probably man-made.

MORE SURPRISES!

★ If you'd like to sponge paint lots of different colors on your shirt, you need more paint and a few more pieces of cut sponge — one for each color. Let dry before adding a new color. After the first color has dried, you can paint over the same area, or on a different place on your shirt.

★ Instead of using contact paper for your design, you can cut the sponges into the shapes you want and apply directly onto paper or fabric. Press and lift without smudging.

★ To make gift wrap, cut sponges into shapes and sponge paint one color at a time onto a roll of plain paper or butcher paper.

Travel Hunt

There's no reason to be bored on a trip. There are plenty of shapes to hunt for to help time fly by and to help you see a lot more around you!

AGES 3-6

HERE'S WHAT YOU DO

1. Ask a grown-up to fold your paper into eighths. Cut the sections apart.

2. Ask a grown-up to write down eight things you will be able to see on your trip including three shapes, two letters, two colors, and one number — one on each piece of paper. Fold each paper and put in the bag. Your Travel Hunt Bag is now ready to go!

3. While you're on your way, open the bag and pull out one slip of paper. What's on it? Can you find that shape or color? When you find it, leave that slip out and choose another from the bag. You've won the game when the bag is empty!

From Here to There

Can you think of different ways to travel? Some involve only your body, others use animals, while others need machines. Some are on land, some on or under water, and some are in the air.

★ Want to make the game more difficult? Along with each shape or color, tell how many times you must find it (like four squares or five red objects).

★ Look for specific objects such as four blue cars or three dogs. The more specific, the harder it will be to spot things.

★ Keep your eyes open and become a travel detective! Try to stump your travel companions by asking them questions like what color was the house we just passed? Were there any cars in the driveway? What kind of animals are in that field? What number is on that sign?

Shape Detective

HERE'S WHAT YOU NEED

Plain paper

Pencil or crayon

Guess what you'll be looking for if you're a Shape Detective? You'll be hunting for circles, squares, triangles, and rectangles — in the strangest places!

HERE'S WHAT YOU DO

1 Down the left hand margin of a sheet of paper, draw a circle, square, triangle, and rectangle. Carefully study each shape.

2 Now, it's time to become a Shape Detective and go on a Shape Hunt! Walk slowly through each room in your home. Each time you find something that matches one of the shapes on your paper, make a check mark next to that shape. Here's a hint to start: Look carefully at the doors — can you recognize what shape they are?

3 When you've traveled through the whole building, you've finished your Shape Hunt. Count up all of the shapes you found. Which shape did you find the most times? Which did you find the least? How many shapes did you find altogether?

ALIKE AND DIFFERENT

Shapes can be sneaky! If you turn them upside-down or on their side, some shapes can look very different. Try looking at your drawing of each shape as you rotate the page.

HELPING · HANDS

Shape Detective is an excellent visual discrimination activity in which children pick out shapes hidden in common objects. Beginning detectives may want to focus on only one shape at a time.

Plenty of Patterns

AGES 4-6

It's fun to draw shapes. How would you like to make your very own deck of pattern cards?

HERE'S WHAT YOU DO

1 Have a grown-up draw four or five simple shapes, such as a triangle, square, circle, rectangle, and star, one on each 3" x 5" card. Now, you copy each shape onto a blank card.

2 This time your partner will hold up each card, and then turn it face down. Can you draw the shape without looking? (If not, take a peek.)

3 You draw some shapes on cards for your partner to copy.

HELPING • HANDS Some children will not be able to draw from memory; that's not a problem. You can also play Make-A-Match by mixing pairs of cards together, and laying them out face down. Take turns choosing two cards: if they match, keep them; if not, put them back. The winner is the player with the most matches.

Lots of Colors

Whirls and swirls of colors are all around you — in autumn trees, spring flowers, cars whizzing by, and your favorite shirt! Color makes life exciting. It's fun to play with colors.

Tissue Paper Rainbow

Tissue paper comes in all colors and patterns and makes great wrapping paper for gifts. Let's see what else you can do with it.

AGES 2-6

HERE'S WHAT YOU NEED

Various colors of tissue paper

White construction paper

Glue

Pencil

HERE'S WHAT YOU DO

1 Draw a rainbow on the construction paper. Tear the tissue paper into lots of small pieces.

2 Spread a little glue on one band of your rainbow. Press one color of tissue paper pieces onto the glue. Then, cover the other bands of your rainbow with glue and tissue paper pieces. Let your Tissue Paper Rainbow dry.

To avoid sticky fingers and messy projects, squeeze a small puddle of glue onto scrap paper and provide toothpicks for easy spreading.

MY FLOWER GARDEN

GLUE

MORE SURPRISES!

★ Pick up a sheet of tissue paper and look through it. What do you see? Now look through another color. Which tissue paper color is your favorite to look through?

★ Cut out shapes and patterns from a sheet of construction paper and cover the holes with tissue paper. Glue them in place for a suncatcher to hang in your bedroom window!

★ Crumple up pieces of different-colored tissue paper and glue them on paper. Draw on stems and leaves for a paper flower garden!

Shaving Cream Pictures

What's squishy, soft, fluffy, white, looks like a cloud, and is fun to touch and play with? Shaving cream! And just wait until you see what you can do with it!

 AGES 2-6

HELPING • HANDS

You may have to join in so that children will know that it is okay to be messy when drawing Shaving Cream Pictures.

HERE'S WHAT YOU DO

1. Wear a smock and cover a table or an area outside with a plastic tablecloth. Squirt a blob of shaving cream onto the tablecloth. Pick a color and sprinkle a little bit of tempera paint powder into the shaving cream and mix with your hands.

2. Spread the shaving cream thinly on the tablecloth. Use your finger to draw a circle or square, a person, a house, a puppy, some wiggly lines, or big swirls.

3. Mix up a second and third color shaving cream blob. Try mixing some of the colors together to form new colors or to form streaks of color.

4. To clean up, just wash off the tablecloth and your hands with soap and water.

MORE SURPRISES!

★ Mix up small blobs of red, yellow, and blue shaving cream and tempera powder. Now carefully combine a dab from the red and blue blobs. What color do you get? What color do you get when you combine a dab from the red and yellow blobs? The blue and yellow?

★ Create a three-dimensional shaving cream drawing by fluffing up the cream.

★ Write your name in the shaving cream. If you make a mistake, what do you think you can use as an eraser?

★ Make shaving cream drawings outdoors in the summertime. Wear your bathing suit and then clean up by playing under the hose.

Coffee Can Color Sort

AGES 3-5

Want to have double fun? First make this game and then play it!

HERE'S WHAT YOU NEED

- Coffee cans or other containers
- Construction paper: red, blue, and yellow
- Safety scissors
- Pencil and tape
- Cardboard templates for circle, square, triangle

HERE'S WHAT YOU DO

1. Trace two of each shape on each color of construction paper.

2. Cut out each of the shapes. (You will have six of each shape.)

3. Cut out a piece of each color paper, and tape one color on each coffee can.

4. Now, mix all your shapes together. Then, sort all the colored shapes into their own colored coffee can. Then, dump the shapes out, mix them all up, and sort them again!

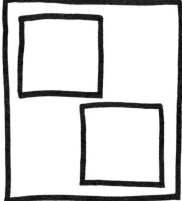

CUT OUT PAPER SHAPES

TAPE A COLOR ON EACH CAN

MORE SURPRISES!

★ This time sort by shape. Put the circles in one can, the squares in another, and the triangles in the third.

★ Now, use your sense of touch to sort. Close your eyes and feel the shapes with your fingers to sort — without looking! Is it possible to sort by color with your eyes closed?

HELPING • HANDS

Color Sort not only helps children recognize colors; simple sorting activities help them begin to compare and categorize.

Color Walk

Look around you, and what do you see? Lots of wonderful colors!
Let's go for a walk and see what colors you can find.

HERE'S WHAT YOU NEED

Crayons

Paper

HERE'S WHAT YOU DO

1 Choose one color that you would like to hunt for on a Color Walk. You can call it your "Color for the Day!"

2 Walk around indoors looking for things that have your "Color for the Day." You might have to look in a drawer, or under a table, or in a closet to find your color.

3 After you've searched indoors, get ready to go outside with a grown-up to look for your "Color for the Day." Remember to look all around you: the sky, the trees, the ground, birds...all sorts of things might have your color.

4 When you return, draw a picture of some of the things you found. Be sure to use the crayon that is your "Color for the Day."

HELPING · HANDS

Color Walk can be done again and again, focusing on a different color each time. Vary the places that you walk and encourage each child to be a careful observer.

MORE SURPRISES!

★ Celebrate your color of the day! Dress in that color, eat snacks in that color, paint a picture in that color, or make a paper chain in shades of that color.

★ Colors have different shades — everything from dark to light and lots of shades in-between. Go on a Color Hunt, looking for things in different shades of the same color, like all the red things or blue things you can find. Then line them up from the **darkest** to the **lightest**.

★ Take a survey of people's favorite colors. Ask your friends and family members which is their favorite color. Do any of them have the same favorite as you?

Racing Colors

Which of these three colors do you think can win a race: red, blue, or yellow?

HERE'S WHAT YOU NEED

3 small toy cars or 3 coins

White construction paper

Scrap paper

Crayons

Paper lunch bag

On your mark, get set, GO!

"On your mark" really means *take your places*, which is something that's important for people in a race to do. Can you think of other words to start people off in a race?

HERE'S WHAT YOU DO

1. Ask a grown-up to help you make a game board: Draw two parallel lines down the length of a sheet of construction paper. Label one end START and the other end FINISH, and then draw five circles from start to finish down each lane. Color all the circles in the first lane red, the second lane yellow, and the third lane blue.

2. Tear or cut three small pieces from a sheet of paper. Color one piece red, one blue, and one yellow. Put all three slips in a lunch bag. You're ready to play!

3. Line up the cars at START, one in each lane. Draw one slip of paper from the bag. The color on the board that matches the slip of paper tells you which car to move. Move that car up one spot. Put the slip of paper back in the bag, shake it up, and draw again. Keep playing until one of the cars reaches the FINISH. That car is the winner!

LANE 1 COLOR CIRCLES RED
LANE 2 COLOR CIRCLES YELLOW
LANE 3 COLOR CIRCLES BLUE

START

FINISH

RED
BLUE
YELLOW
COLOR 3 PAPER PIECES AND PUT THEM IN A PAPER BAG

MORE SURPRISES!

★ Invite two friends to play with you. Each player can choose a color, and take turns in order. See who's color wins the most races.

★ When traveling, pick a color and count the number of cars you see in that color.

HELPING • HANDS

Make different game boards using new colors as each child's knowledge of colors expands. Older children may enjoy additional circles and more color lines on the game board.

Ice Painting

AGES 3-6

Ice cube paintbrushes
(see step #1)

Tempera paint powder,
several colors

Spoon

Heavy paper

We use ice to cool down a drink, to skate on, and to keep food cold, but did you ever hear of anyone using an ice cube as a paintbrush?

HERE'S WHAT YOU DO

1 To make an ice cube paintbrush, poke Popsicle sticks into partially frozen ice cubes. Then, continue to freeze solid.

2 Take an ice cube paintbrush by its handle and rub it back and forth over the powdered color on the paper. What happens?

3 Try putting small amounts of other colors on your paper and rubbing those with another ice cube paintbrush. What happens if you swirl two colors together? See if you can make a very colorful painting!

4 When you are finished, leave your paper on the table to dry. Now you have a special picture to hang in your room!

HELPING · HANDS To avoid paper rips, replace the paper before each work of art becomes too wet.

Amazing Alphabet

With the 26 letters in the alphabet, you can spell your name, write "I love you" to a friend, or listen to the words in your favorite story. Do you know what letter your name begins with?

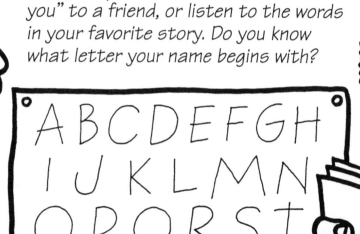

A B C D E F G H
I J K L M N
O P Q R S T
U V W X Y Z

ABC Cookies

 AGES 2-6

What can you *do* with the letters of the alphabet? Well, you can look at them, trace them, draw and touch them, put them together to form words — but did you know that you can eat them, too?

HERE'S WHAT YOU DO

1. After washing your hands, ask a grown-up to help you measure out the shortening, sugar, anise flavoring, eggs, and vanilla into a bowl.

2. Help mix these ingredients to a creamy consistency. Add flour and baking powder, a little at a time. A grown-up can use the mixer on low to combine these ingredients each time you add more.

3. Sprinkle flour on the kitchen table, and scoop out dough (add a little more flour, if sticky). Break off a bit of dough and roll it with both hands into a dough rope.

4. Choose a letter of the alphabet that you'd like to learn (perhaps the first letter of your name). A grown-up can roll a dough rope and make that letter. Now, you copy it. As you make each letter, say it aloud and place it on a cookie sheet.

5. A grown-up can bake your cookies in a 350° F (180° C) oven for 12 to 15 minutes. After they've cooled, choose your favorite letter to eat. Now you can tell your friends that you ate a letter today!

MORE SURPRISES!

★ Add some color to your cookies! Separate the dough into three sections. Add a few drops of different food coloring to each. Work the color into the dough by squeezing and squashing it with your hands.

★ With more practice, children can make their initials or spell out their whole names. For a birthday surprise, spell out the guest of honor's name in colorful cookie dough!

HELPING·HANDS

Kitchen fun is a great way to learn, but it also demands careful supervision and advance planning.

Trace-A-Letter

AGES 3-6

Wouldn't it be fun to draw letters if you could use a magic pencil and eraser? Guess what — you can! Your finger will be the magic pencil, and sand will be your magic eraser. Are you ready to try some magic writing?

HERE'S WHAT YOU DO

1 Cover the bottom of a pie pan with sand, sugar, or oatmeal.

2 Ask a grown-up to draw a letter in the pan. Trace over it with your magic pencil (your finger) and say its name aloud.

3 To magically erase your letter, smooth the sand so it covers the bottom again. Now try drawing the letter by yourself, saying its name.

Great Games

Ask a grown-up to write letters and shapes on different pieces of paper. Put the pieces of paper in a bowl. Now, you and a friend take turns removing a piece of paper from the bowl, drawing the letter or shape in the pan of sand, and guessing what each drew.

MORE SURPRISES!

★ Trace around a yogurt container to make a circle, or a small milk carton to make a square. Then, try making the shape without the container.

★ Spell your name in the sand. Instead of a pie pan, use a cookie sheet to give you lots of room for a whole word.

★ Go to the beach and write messages in the sand.

HELPING HANDS

Start simple. You may need to direct the drawing finger at first. Be sure to always say the name of what you are drawing.

Bean Fun

AGES 3-6

Dried beans can be used to grow plants, make soups and stews — and make unusual alphabet art, too!

BY ME

HERE'S WHAT YOU NEED

- Dried beans
- Paper and pencil
- Glue
- Newspaper

HELPING • HANDS

Larger beans like kidney beans and lima beans work best for little hands. Of course, supervise closely when working with toddlers.

HERE'S WHAT YOU DO

1. Cover the table with newspaper. On a piece of paper, draw a new letter you are learning. Then, for fun, draw a big shape around it, such as an "R" inside a triangle.

2. Spread glue along the letter. Place the beans on the glue, as close together as you can place them. Now you have a bean letter.

3. Next, outline the shape in glue. Again, glue the beans close together.

Bean Art

To make bean flower art, squeeze a small amount of glue on a piece of construction paper. Glue several beans to the center of your paper for the flower center. Glue other beans, dried peas, or dried pumpkin seeds around the center to make petals. Use twigs or yarn to glue on a stem and leaves.

MORE SURPRISES!

★ Before you begin, sort your beans into light-colored and dark-colored beans. Then make your letter out of one pile and your shape out of another.

★ Close your eyes and run your fingers over your bean art. Does feeling it with your fingers help you picture it in your mind?

★ Listen to these bean fairy tales: *Jack and the Beanstalk, The Princess and the Pea* by Hans Christian Anderson, and *The Straw, The Coal, and The Bean* by the Brothers Grimm.

Body Letters

AGES 4-6

All twenty-six letters of the alphabet are made up of straight lines, curved lines, or a little of both. To make some alphabet shapes with your body, you can stand up straight as a pencil or bend over and curve to the floor.

HERE'S WHAT YOU NEED

An alphabet book

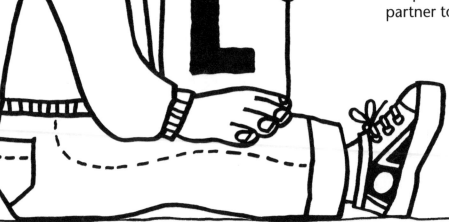

HERE'S WHAT YOU DO

1. Find a picture of the letter "L" or the letter "T." Those are both straight-line letters. Can you make your body look like an "L," and then like a "T"? Is it easier to do with a partner?

2. Now, try a curved letter like a "C."

3. Find a picture of your favorite letter. Is it made up of curves, straight lines, or a combination of both? Try to make your body match the picture, or work with a partner to make the letter.

Sign It

American Sign Language is used by people who are hearing impaired. It involves making words and letters with hand and arm movements. You can learn some of these letters, too!

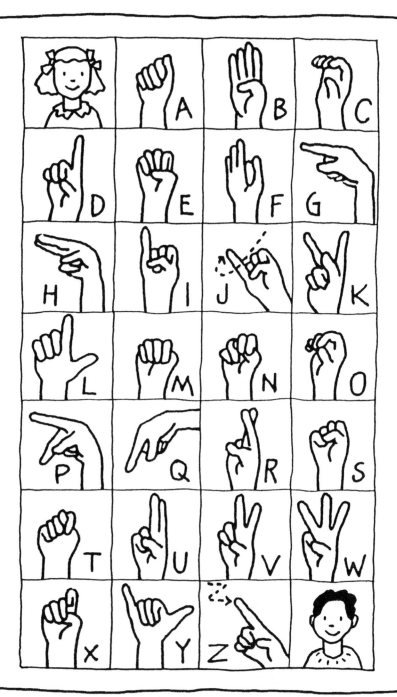

★ Play an alphabet game. Ask a partner to make his or her body into a letter of the alphabet. Can you tell what the letter is? Ask for a hint if you aren't sure.

HELPING • HANDS

As children make different letters, talk with them about how the letter is shaped, and whether it involves curved lines, straight lines, or both. This helps reinforce visual memory of the letter. The body movement also helps to reinforce learning of the alphabet. To minimize confusion, play with only three or four letters at a time.

Palm Drawings

AGES 4-6

You can recognize letters by the way they look. Here's a fun game that shows another way to recognize letters — through your palms, fingertips, and your sense of touch!

HERE'S WHAT YOU NEED

A partner

HERE'S WHAT YOU DO

1 Face your partner, put your hand out palm up, and close your eyes. Your partner softly draws a letter on your palm with his or her finger for you to try and guess. It may tickle just a little!

2 As your partner slowly traces a letter, keep your eyes closed and try to picture the letter in your mind. Ask for a clue to help you out.

MORE SURPRISES!

★ Would you like to know some other ways to "feel" the alphabet? Ask a partner to lightly trace the letters of the alphabet, one at a time, on your back!

★ Want to trace a word or message in your partner's hand? Here are some that make up a very special message: I-L-O-V-E-Y-O-U.

HELPING · HANDS

If a child has difficulty recognizing letters with closed eyes, ask him or her to watch as you trace the letter. Say the letter, too, as you draw. The extra sensory input can be very helpful.

Make-A-Match

AGES 4-6

Your eyes can help you tell which things are alike and which are different. Here is a fun way to match pairs of letters.

HERE'S WHAT YOU DO

1 Draw two of each of the letters in your name, writing one letter on each card. (A grown-up can draw them in lightly so you can trace over them.)

2 Lay out the letters of your name in order. Match each of the remaining letters by laying them right above each of the letters in your name. Now, you have spelled your name twice! Mix them up and do it again.

3 Make cards for other letters that you know. If you already know all of the alphabet, start with the letter "A" and make two cards for each letter all the way through "Z." Then play matching letters.

MORE SURPRISES!

★ Here's a chance to use your imagination! Use a pencil or pen to turn each letter into something new! Maybe the letter "A," for example, could become a tepee. What could you turn a "B" into?

★ Make five pairs of matching letters. Then, turn them all face down and play Memory, trying to match up all five pairs.

Sense It!

Your eyes help you to tell the difference between the letters of the alphabet. You have other senses in addition to sight that can help you learn: touch, taste, hearing, and smell. What sense would help you recognize a song on the radio? Tell the difference between perfume and baby powder?

HELPING • HANDS

Make-A-Match lays a good foundation for learning the alphabet. Save time and frustration by making matching alphabet decks in advance. Children can trace over penciled letters with a crayon, and then play matching and memory games.

A B C D E F G

Count Me In! ★

How many fingers do you have? If you can have three cookies for dessert, how do you know when you've had your share? How many toys do you have? When you learn to count, you can answer lots of questions!

Egg Carton Count

AGES 2-6

What can you do with an egg carton? Lots of things, including using it to count!

Empty egg carton

12 small stones or other small objects

1 Gather together your set of 12 small stones. As you count each number out loud, place one stone in each cup of the egg holder. Did you have just the right number of holders for the stones?

2 This time mix up the 12 stones. What will happen now if you put one stone in each egg cup?

3 Now, set two stones aside. Put the remaining stones in the egg cups, one per cup. Will you have **too many stones**, **too many cups**, or **just the right amount**? If you count the number of stones now, how many will you have? Is that number **more** or **fewer** than the number of egg cups?

Egg Carton Maracas

Pour a handful of dried beans into the empty carton and seal it up with masking tape. Shake it and listen: You've created a new musical instrument! Listen to your favorite music and shake your Egg Carton Maracas — and your whole body, too — to the beat of the music.

HELPING · HANDS

Use half an egg carton for children who are just learning to count. Egg Carton Count can provide a format for practicing fine motor and verbal skills, and learning a little bit about one-to-one correspondence.

MORE SURPRISES!

★ What are some foods besides eggs that could fit into each egg cup? What foods are small enough to fit? Would breakfast cereal flakes fit? Peanuts? Apples? How about pretzels? Try putting each into the cups, and see if you guessed right. Now you can have a snack!

★ Use your imagination to think of some other uses for your egg carton. You can be silly (a bathtub for twelve worms), or serious (a place to store shoelaces). What if you turned it upside down or sideways — what could it be used for then?

Face Fun

AGES 2-4

Even though everyone has similar features (like eyes, a nose, and a mouth), we all look different from each other. That makes each of us "one-of-a-kind"!

HERE'S WHAT YOU NEED

Magazines

Mirror

Safety scissors

Glue

Paper

HERE'S WHAT YOU DO

1 Cut out magazine pictures of people's faces. Lay the faces out in front of you. How many eyes in each picture? How many mouths in each picture? How many noses on each face? How many ears on each head?

2 Look at your eyes, nose, mouth, and ears in the mirror. Compare them with the pictures you cut out. Do you have the same number as the pictures do?

ALIKE AND DIFFERENT

Look at a picture of a dog. What is **alike** about a person and a dog? What is **different**? Do people and dogs have the **same number** of eyes, ears, noses, mouths? Can you picture a dog with a nose like yours, or yourself with a dog's ears? That would look silly! Draw your own silly critter.

HELPING • HANDS

Use Face Fun to practice both counting and one-to-one correspondence, as well as descriptive vocabulary practice.

Stop and Think!

In a lot of your books, there are faces on all sorts of things. You can find a train with a face in the book *The Little Engine That Could*. Does that mean that a train has happy and sad feelings like you do?

MY SILLY CRITTER

MORE SURPRISES!

★ Put on a happy face. Besides having a great big smile, what else happens to your face when you're happy? How do your eyes look? Try a sad look. What parts of your face change?

★ Cover your mouth with your hand and make a happy face, then a sad one. Ask a friend to tell which face is which just by looking at your eyes.

★ Ask a partner to sit across from you and pretend to feel happy, sad, surprised, frightened, angry, or excited. Can you tell what feeling your friend is expressing by the look on his or her face?

Count-and-Eat Jewelry

AGES 2-6

This jewelry is special because you can use part of it for a snack!

HERE'S WHAT YOU NEED

Cheerios™

Yarn

HERE'S WHAT YOU DO

1 Put a small piece of tape around one end of the yarn, and tie a large knot on the other end.

2 Pick up one piece of cereal at a time and string it on the yarn, counting each piece you string on. When you have lots of cereal on the yarn, ask a grown-up to tie the ends together so you can slide it loosely over your head. Your necklace is ready to wear . . . and to eat!

3 During the day, snack on your cereal necklace. Are you hungry enough to eat four pieces? Six pieces? Ten pieces? Count how many pieces are left.

Wearable Art

What other foods make good jewelry? Paint uncooked macaroni with water-colors, dry, and string on yarn for beautiful bracelets and necklaces. (Don't eat uncooked macaroni, of course!) Make a necklace of macaroni and Cheerios™ for something extra special.

WRAP A PIECE OF TAPE AROUND ONE END OF YARN

MAKE A KNOT ON OTHER END OF YARN

PAINT MACARONI WITH WATERCOLORS

MORE SURPRISES!

★ Pour a small dish of Cheerios™ or other cereal. Guess how many pieces are in the dish. Then, with the help of a grown-up, count the pieces and see how close you came in your estimate. Did you think there were **more** pieces or **fewer** pieces?

HELPING HANDS Touch each piece of cereal as it is counted in each activity.

Jumping Numbers

AGES 2-6

Find the numbers — using your feet!

HERE'S WHAT YOU NEED

- **Plain paper**
- **Masking tape**
- **Dark marker or crayon**

HERE'S WHAT YOU DO

1 Write the numbers one through ten, one per page, so that each number fills up an entire sheet of paper. (Ask a grown-up to write the number in pencil so you can trace over it with a marker.)

2 Tape your numbers on the floor, about two to three feet apart, in order from one to ten.

3 Jump to each number, starting with one and ending at ten. Then, take turns with a friend calling out any number from one to ten and jumping to it. Jumping Numbers is fun!

Jumping Numbers combines lots of movement with practice in recognizing and counting numbers. It involves multiple senses in the learning process: looking, listening, and moving. Enjoy the interaction and put the focus on fun!

Silly Sayings

That's using your head!

If you do a good job of thinking or solving a problem, people might say to you, "That's using your head!" They say that because your brain — the part of you that does the thinking — is inside your head. In Jumping Numbers, you could say that you're using your head — and your feet!

★ Instead of just jumping to each number, pretend you're a bunny and hop on both feet. Or, pretend to be an ant and crawl to each number. You could even pretend to be a dump truck, "beeping" as you back up to each number. What else can you pretend to be?

★ If you have one or two dice available, you can play a different way. Tape a page 11 and a page 12 to the floor. Each time you roll the dice, count the dots and hop to that number on the floor.

★ If you like to hop, skip, or jump, here's another great game. Ask a friend to roll two dice, count the number of dots, and call out any of the following for you to do that many times: jump, hop on one foot, run, jumping jacks, hip wiggles, toe taps, or hand claps.

Number Puzzles

 AGES 3-6

Puzzles are fun to do, and these are extra special because they're all about numbers!

HELPING·HaNDS

Number Puzzles is a hands-on method of helping your child to associate the number symbols we use with the numbers they represent. For very young children, two puzzles may be enough.

HERE'S WHAT YOU DO

1 Cut the cardboard into five 5" x 7" rectangles. Down the center of each rectangle, draw a wiggly line.

2 On the left side of each rectangle, write the number "1" on the first puzzle, "2" on the second puzzle, and so on up to "5."

3 On the right hand side of the "1" puzzle, glue down one textured item. On the right hand side of the "2" puzzle, glue down two textured objects. Continue until you have all the puzzles completed. Let glue dry.

4 Cut each puzzle apart along the wiggly line so that you have two pieces. Mix them up and try putting them together by matching the written numbers with the number of objects. To be sure you don't miss any, touch each object as you count it.

CUT APART ALONG THE WIGGLY LINE ON EACH CARD

The Magic Touch

Although we use our eyes and ears the most, we have other senses, such as touch, that help us to learn about the world around us. Try doing Number Puzzles with your eyes closed. Have a friend call out a number, and you find the puzzle piece by counting the glued objects.

Paper Chain Counting Calendar

Make a counting calendar so you can count how many days until... your birthday, or Grandma visits, or you go to the beach, or whatever you are looking forward to!

AGES 3-6

HELPING • HANDS

The Paper Chain Counting Calendar is a simple way to make the concept of time and days more concrete for children. For young children, have them make the chain within a week or two of the special date. Use this activity over and over as special events approach.

MY SPECIAL DAY

HERE'S WHAT YOU DO

1 Use your family calendar to count how many days until your special day arrives (like ten days until your birthday). Each link of the chain represents one day.

2 To make a paper chain, cut two or more colors of construction paper into 2" x 8" strips. Tape the ends of one strip together, slide the second strip through the first, and tape it together. Continue adding one strip for each day you want to count.

3 Hang the chain within easy reach. Each morning, tear off one link, and count the links that are left. On the morning you remove the last link, it will be your special day!

CUT 2" x 8" PAPER STRIPS

TAPE ENDS OF STRIPS TOGETHER

ADD A STRIP FOR EACH DAY

LAST LINK IS FOR YOUR SPECIAL DAY

MORE SURPRISES!

★ Now that you know how to make a chain, create a very long chain to decorate your room.

★ Want to use a grown-up calendar? Ask if you can mark your special day on a calendar in bright colors. Then, put an X on today's date. Each day, put an X on the next date. To see how many more days you have to wait, just count the days between the X's and your special day!

Silly Sayings

There's no time like the present.

How could time be like a present all wrapped up in a box? Do you think that's what this means? Actually, the word *present* also means *right now*. So, there's no time like right now — to have fun, ask a question, or help someone.

Creative Creatures

AGES 4-6

Use your imagination and the roll of the dice to make these funny creatures look very unusual, indeed!

HERE'S WHAT YOU DO

1. In the center of your sheet of paper, draw a body for your creature in any shape you want — a circle, a square, a triangle, peanut-shaped, or squiggly.

2. Decide what you'd like to add next: arms, legs, heads, feet, tails ... you get the idea. Roll the dice and count how many dots are showing. If you chose to draw legs, and rolled a five, you'd draw five legs on your creature.

3. Roll the dice for each body part, including details like how many eyes, ears, noses, mouths, fingers, and toes your creature will have.

4. Color your creation and hang up your picture.

HELPING · HANDS

This activity helps children to practice both counting and fine motor skills in a creative and fun way.

MORE SURPRISES!

★ Make a whole family of count-the-dot creations.

★ Make up a story about your creature. Where does it come from and what does it eat?

ROLL THE DICE FOR EACH BODY PART

A Counting Pictograph

Did you know that everything around you can be counted, from the number of clouds in the sky to the number of teeth in your mouth? Let's pick a few things to count.

AGES 4-6

HERE'S WHAT YOU NEED

Glue

Colored construction paper

White paper

Crayons

Safety scissors

HERE'S WHAT YOU DO

1 Choose two or three things that you'd like to count. You might count all the tooth-brushes in the bathroom, then combs, then towels.

2 Now, make a pictograph. If you counted six tooth-brushes, draw each tooth-brush on the white paper and color. Cut out each toothbrush. Glue your tooth-brushes in a line across the top of the construction paper.

3 Now, do the same thing with the combs you counted, carefully making a second row so that each comb is directly beneath one tooth-brush. Repeat, gluing the towels in the third row.

4 Count each row of pictures. Which row has the **most**? Which one has the **fewest**? Does your pictograph tell you which has the most and which has the fewest without counting?

MORE SURPRISES!

★ If you have some building blocks, make a Counting Tower by counting each block as you stack it.

★ Can you think of other things to stack up and count? How about pennies? What about pillows? If you have a stack of five marshmallows and another stack of five napkins, which one do you think will be taller? Try it and see!

★ Make a pictograph in the sand of things you count at the beach.

HELPING • HANDS

This activity travels well; you can transport the idea to a nature walk (how many red flowers, caterpillars, clouds in the sky) or a trip to the zoo. Encourage each child to make a graph of the counted objects for a concrete representation of what was seen.

BLOCKS

BUTTONS

PILLOWS

Sort It Out! ⭐

To sort something is to arrange it into groups — by size, texture (how it feels), color, shape, taste, use, and more. If you put all your small toys in one place or eat all the red jelly beans, then guess what? You already know how to sort!

Big and Small

AGES 2-4

Did you know that sorting is an important part of many different jobs? Mail delivery people sort the mail every day to be sure it goes to the right house. Grocers sort the food on their shelves so it's easy for people to find. Would you like to learn how to sort?

HERE'S WHAT YOU NEED

5 or 6 plastic containers, varied sizes

HERE'S WHAT YOU DO

1 Look carefully at the containers. Which one is the largest? Set that container on the table in front of you.

2 Keep adding one container at a time, placing each one in order of size from smallest to largest, until you've used them all. How many containers did you sort by size?

3 Now that they're in order, try stacking the smaller ones inside the larger ones. How many can you fit into the largest container?

Musical Containers

● Make a container drum: Just put the lid on one container and use a spoon as your drumstick. Drum the beat as you sing a song.

● Make container shakers: Put a handful of buttons or dried rice in a plastic container, and put the lid on. Pick up your new instrument and shake, rattle, and roll!

DRUM

←LID

←LARGE CONTAINER

SHAKER

BUTTONS

CONTAINER LID

SMALL CONTAINER

Mort Loves to Sort

There once was a boy named Mort
Who didn't know how to sort.
And then he found out
What sorting's about;
Now Mort thinks that sorting's a sport.

★ Can you put these items in order by size from smallest to largest: a cracker, a banana, a rubber band, and a paper clip? Can you add any more objects to make an even longer row of small to large items?

★ Do you think that a small plastic container would make a good bed for a mouse? Could it be used as a swimming pool for a baby duck? What unusual uses for plastic containers can you think of?

HELPING · HANDS

To expand this activity, introduce new items for the children to sort.

Food Sort

There sure are a lot of different kinds of foods at the grocery store. How do you think the grocer decided where to place each food on the shelves?

AGES 2-6

HERE'S WHAT YOU NEED

Bags of groceries, or some foods from cupboards

HERE'S WHAT YOU DO

1 Empty the groceries onto the kitchen table. How might you group the foods? One way to divide the foods into two groups is according to foods you like and foods you don't like.

2 Can you group the foods according to how each is packaged — cans, boxes, jars, or bags? Try it and see!

3 Try sorting the food by its temperature: Is it frozen, cold, or room temperature?

HELPING • HANDS

Encourage each child to explain why a food is placed in a particular category. This helps to clarify logic and practice speaking skills.

Silly Sayings

Life is a bowl of cherries!

How could life be like a bowl of cherries? Well, picture a cherry: It has a sweet, red outside and a hard pit inside. Now think about the good parts of each day and the more difficult parts. How is life like a bowl of cherries?

★ Try other ways to sort the same groceries. Sort by which meal they are usually eaten at: breakfast, lunch, or dinner. Or sort by taste: sweet, sour, or spicy. Then, sort by color.

★ Here's a sorting challenge: Sort by whether the groceries are meat, vegetable, fruit, or a nonfood item like paper towels.

★ Play Food Pairs: Two things that are the same are called a pair, like a pair of socks or a pair of mittens. Try to find any foods or packages that are the same — like two boxes of cereal or two apples. How many pairs of food items can you find?

★ Sort the foods into piles: those that go in the refrigerator, in the cupboard, in the pantry. See how sorting helps you to be organized!

Imagination Station

Toys are for playing with, right? Here's an idea for a new way that you can have lots of fun with your toys.

 AGES 2-6

HERE'S WHAT YOU NEED

Some toys

Your imagination!

HERE'S WHAT YOU DO

1 Spread out the toys in front of you. Pick out the biggest toy and the smallest toy. Now sort all of the toys by size.

2 Next, sort the toys by texture (how they feel — soft, rough, hard). Make two piles, one for "soft toys" and one for "hard toys." Which do you have more of?

3 Now, sort the toys by use, like toys for building and toys with wheels, or hugging toys and action figures.

ALIKE AND DIFFERENT

The things you sorted are alike because they're toys. But they're different, too. Their color, size, shape, texture, and how you play with them can be different. If all of your toys were exactly alike, they wouldn't be much fun to play with, would they? It's the differences that make toys and people interesting and fun!

MORE SURPRISES!

★ After you've sorted the toys, make some toy organizers. On the outside of each box, draw a picture of what kind of toys you'll be putting in that box. The next time you are ready to play with your toys, you will know just where they are!

★ Take all the parts and pieces of old games and broken toys and see what you can create from the odds and ends. Let your imagination be your guide!

HELPING HANDS

Use Imagination Station to encourage organizational skills and to prompt children to put away toys at end of playtime.

Animal Round-Up

AGES 3-6

Animals are fun to look at, listen to, and learn about! Let's use some of what you already know about animals in a different way.

BIG · LITTLE · FURRY ANIMALS

Picture books of animals

Paper

Crayons

HERE'S WHAT YOU DO

1 Select some books with lots of pictures of animals. As you look through the books, name all the animals you can think of that have fur. A dog has fur, a bear has fur; how many other animals can you name that have fur?

2 Now, look at the pictures and name all of the animals that fit into these other groups: animals that are big, animals that are small, animals with four legs, animals with two legs, animals that live near water, and animals with feathers. Some of the same animals will fit into many different groups.

ALIKE AND DIFFERENT

What is one thing that is alike about a horse and a mouse? What is one thing that's different about a horse and a mouse? Take turns with a friend finding out what is alike and what is different about some of your favorite animals.

HELPING · HANDS

By helping children discover many different ways to sort and categorize the same animals, you will help them build flexibility into their thinking.

MORE SURPRISES!

★ What is your favorite animal? What does it eat and where does it sleep?

★ Cut out parts of different animals from old magazines. Glue them together to create an entirely new animal and then make up a story about your new animal.

★ Find some picture books about dinosaurs in the library. See if you can discover which were big, which were small, which ate meat, which were plant eaters, which had four feet, and which had only two. Can you think of some other groups to put dinosaurs in?

Memories Box

AGES 3-6

It's a lot of fun to remember times that you really enjoyed.

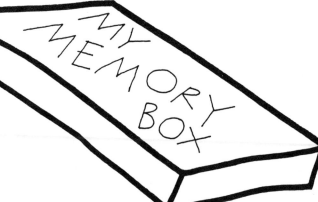

MY MEMORY BOX

HERE'S WHAT YOU DO

1. Cut pieces of construction paper to cover the top and the sides of your Memories Box, and tape them down. Ask a grown-up to help you print your name on the top. Draw pictures or designs on the box.

2. Sort through your things to find special treasures such as photographs, notes, small toys, a special stone, feather, or piece of sea glass to put in your Memories Box.

Silly Sayings

One person's trash is another person's treasure.

What could this mean? Look in your Memories Box. Is there something in there that is special only to you, like a favorite rock that you found at the beach or a piece of yarn that your grandma always kept her keys on? Maybe this silly saying isn't so silly after all.

CUT PAPER TO FIT BOX TOP AND PASTE; THEN WRITE NAME

STEVE

CUT PAPER TO FIT BOX SIDES; THEN PASTE ON BOX

MORE SURPRISES!

★ When you have everything you want for now in your Memories Box, sit down with a friend and look through the box together. You can show your treasures and tell about why each is special to you.

★ Have some photo fun. See how much you've changed by looking at your baby pictures. Sort them by your age or by where you were (put all the beach pictures in one pile, all the photos from Grandpa's house in another).

HELPING HANDS Explore feelings about the treasures by asking questions and listening to what is said.

Dough Bead Necklace

Turn a lump of dough into a bright and colorful necklace — but first sort the colors into a colorful pattern.

AGES 3-6

HERE'S WHAT YOU NEED

3 cups (750 ml) flour

¼ cup (50 ml) salt

1 cup (250 ml) water

1 tablespoon (15 ml) vegetable oil

Food coloring

Yarn

Pencil or wide nail

HELPING · HANDS

Encourage observation and sorting, by looking at different details in each bead — these are red and blue, these are solid colors, these are small, these are larger.

HERE'S WHAT YOU DO

1. Mix together the flour and salt in a bowl. Add the water and oil, mixing well until the dough is formed. Divide dough into three or four clumps. Add several drops of food coloring to each and knead dough until colored evenly.

2. Now you're ready to make some colorful clay beads! Break off a small chunk of clay, about the size of a large marble. Roll it between your hands until it's round to make a bead. Or, to make beads that have swirls of colors, take a small amount of two or three colors of clay and gently roll them together into one bead.

3. Push a pencil through the center of each bead. Set the beads aside to dry for a day or two, or ask a grown-up to bake in a 350° F (180° C) oven for 30 minutes.

4. When the beads are dry, count and sort them by color, size, or design. When you're ready to make a necklace, lay out the beads in the order or pattern you like best. Wrap a piece of tape around one end of the yarn and tie a thick knot in the other end. Thread the beads on the yarn, using lots of beads. Ask a grown-up to loosely tie the ends for you.

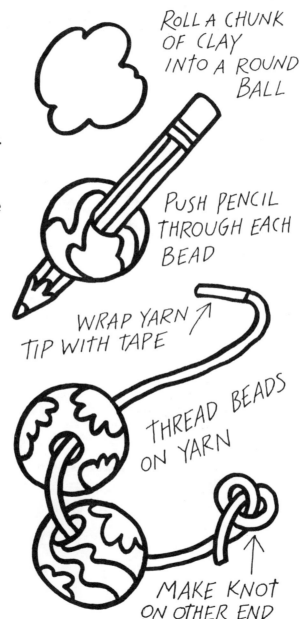

ROLL A CHUNK OF CLAY INTO A ROUND BALL

PUSH PENCIL THROUGH EACH BEAD

WRAP YARN TIP WITH TAPE

THREAD BEADS ON YARN

MAKE KNOT ON OTHER END

MORE SURPRISES!

★ Make Dough Bead Friendship Bracelets. Follow the instructions for necklaces, but only cut the yarn to bracelet size. You make the beads for your friend's bracelet, and your friend will make the beads for yours.

ALIKE AND DIFFERENT

Men and women around the world wear jewelry. Look in magazines and compare your Dough Bead Necklace to other necklaces. All of these are alike because they are worn around the neck. How are they different?

Matching Groups

 AGES 4-6

A beach bucket and sand go together, just as a hat, mittens, scarf, and boots belong together. Have some fun making matching groups.

TRUCK
CAR
MOTORCYCLE
DISH
BUS

HERE'S WHAT YOU NEED

A grown-up partner

HERE'S WHAT YOU DO

1 Ask your partner to list three or four words of items that belong together, and one that doesn't (for example: truck, car, motorcycle, dish, bus).

2 Can you tell which item doesn't belong with the others? Why doesn't it match?

3 Try other groupings. Take turns with your partner naming groups and picking out what doesn't fit.

HELPING • HANDS

Gear the groupings to the level of understanding of each child. Begin with obvious groupings like colors, shapes, transportation types, foods. Encourage children to use their experience and logic to define groups. Sometimes words can be grouped together in ways that aren't obvious.

Let's Compare!

My older sister's big, and my baby brother's small. They are different sizes. A car horn is loud and a whisper is soft. They are different noises. Comparing helps us to look at differences and also to notice how things are alike.

What's That Sound?

AGES 2-6

HERE'S WHAT YOU NEED

A quiet room

Shhhh! Listen! What do you hear? There are lots of sounds all around you every day.

HERE'S WHAT YOU DO

1 Sit quietly in a room and name all the different sounds you can hear.

2 Listen again and name any new sounds that you hear. Is the clock ticking? Is there a bee buzzing? Count all the sounds.

★ Close your eyes and ask a partner to make a noise with a noisemaker like a set of keys, squeaky toy, or crumpling paper. Can you tell what the noise is?

★ Pretend you are a sound machine robot and that people come to you when they want to hear different sounds. Each time they push a button on your hand, you make the sound they ask for. Can you make the sound of a bird chirping? A thunderstorm? The wind blowing?

★ Some sounds make us giggle and some sounds may frighten us. Talk about how different sounds make you feel.

Silly Sayings

Bzzzz

Psssst!

Shhhh!

Some of the sounds around us are fun to hear and fun to make. What other silly sounds can you make?

Mirror Pals

 AGES 2-6

It's fun to stand in front of a mirror and make funny faces or stand in silly poses. Here's another way to get a "mirror image" of what you are doing!

HERE'S WHAT YOU NEED

A large mirror

A partner

HERE'S WHAT YOU DO

1 Try standing on one foot in front of the mirror, jumping up and down and waving your arms. Watch as your reflection does the same things you do — at the same time!

2 Now, play Mirror Pals with a partner. Begin by sitting on the floor facing your partner. Decide who will be the leader. As the leader moves very slowly, the mirror pal moves exactly the same way. The leader can raise an arm, make a sad face, or tap a foot. Take turns being the leader and the mirror pal.

★ Try some of these motions with your mirror pal: wiping a window, eating a bowl of cereal, flying a kite.

★ Practice Mirror Pals with the same partner. Then, ask someone to come watch. See if they can tell who is the leader and who is the mirror.

★ Take turns acting out some everyday activities. Guess what your partner is pretending to do by noticing movements and facial expressions.

HELPING · HANDS

Mirror Pals is both simple to understand and challenging to do. You may want to be the leader at first, doing simple movements slowly. As the mirror pals become more proficient, they can do simple pantomimes like painting a picture or making a sandwich.

Big and Little Day

AGES 2-6

Everything around us has its own size.
Enjoy a special day to celebrate things
that are big and things that are little.

HERE'S WHAT YOU NEED

Old magazines

BIG ELEPHANT

LITTLE ANT

HERE'S WHAT YOU DO

1 Take a big and little walk! Put on some fun marching music and march from room to room. As you march, point to things that are big and say "big!" with a BIG voice. Point to things that are little as you say "little" in a very little voice.

2 Cut out pictures of big things and little things from old magazines. Sort them into big and little piles. Compare all the pictures of big things with each other. Are they all the same size or are some bigger than others? Do the same for the little objects.

3 Play elephant and ant. Pretend to be an elephant. If you were an elephant, what things would seem big to you? (Remember, they would have to be bigger than an elephant!) Now, pretend to be an ant. What things would seem big to you? If an ant was looking at you right now, would it think you were big or little?

MORE SURPRISES!

★ Have a Big Day when you wear big, baggy clothes, eat a big-sized snack, play with your big toys, and draw a picture on a big piece of paper.

★ Put baby pictures on your refrigerator or bulletin board. Then, look in the mirror and see how you have changed from little to big.

In the Bag

AGES 3-6

Find out just how clever your fingers really are!

HERE'S WHAT YOU NEED

Small, common house-hold items like a spoon and paper clip

Paper bag

HERE'S WHAT YOU DO

1 Close your eyes and ask your partner to put an item into a paper bag.

2 Reach into the bag and describe what you feel using words like **smooth, fuzzy, rough, bumpy, hard, soft, solid, round, straight, large, small**.

3 Now, guess what is in the bag. Take a peek. How close was your guess?

4 Take turns with your partner using different items.

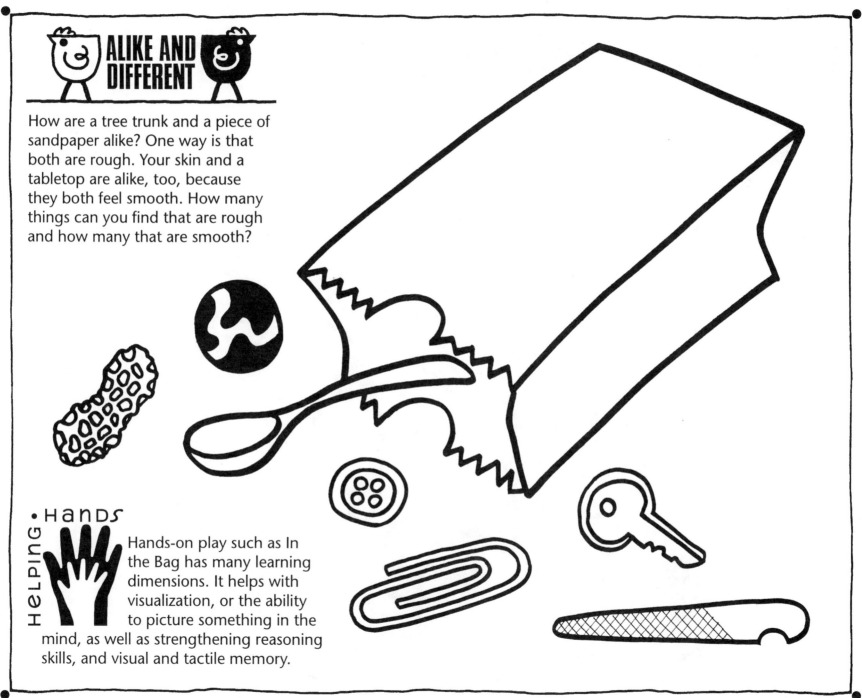

ALIKE AND DIFFERENT

How are a tree trunk and a piece of sandpaper alike? One way is that both are rough. Your skin and a tabletop are alike, too, because they both feel smooth. How many things can you find that are rough and how many that are smooth?

HELPING·HANDS

Hands-on play such as In the Bag has many learning dimensions. It helps with visualization, or the ability to picture something in the mind, as well as strengthening reasoning skills, and visual and tactile memory.

What's Missing?

AGES 3-6

Being a good observer means looking carefully around you. You'll be surprised at how much you actually see!

HERE'S WHAT YOU NEED

3-6 common household items

A handkerchief

HERE'S WHAT YOU DO

1 Ask a partner to place several items on the table or floor for you to look at and touch. Close your eyes while your partner covers one item with the handkerchief.

2 Now, open your eyes and take a good look. Do you know which item has been covered up? To give yourself a hint, reach under the handkerchief and touch what's under it. Now can you remember?

HELPING · HANDS

Since some children are apprehensive about reaching under the handkerchief, suggest peeking underneath before touching the object.

MORE SURPRISES!

★ To become an even more careful observer, place more objects in front of you. This time, ask your partner to remove the object rather than cover it with a hand-kerchief. Now the game is even trickier!

★ Spend a minute or two looking around any room or space carefully. Ask a friend to hide one item that's in plain view while you close your eyes. Then, open your eyes and see if you can tell what's missing!

★ For an exciting adventure, listen to Shel Silverstein's *The Missing Piece* and *The Missing Piece Meets the Big O*.

Self-Portraits

 AGES 3-6

Quick! Without looking, do you know how many eyes you have or what color they are?

ME

HERE'S WHAT YOU DO

1 Lie down on the floor on your back with a sheet of paper under your head. Ask a partner to trace the outline of your head in pencil.

2 Now, draw a self-portrait by filling in the outline with drawings of your eyes, nose, and mouth. Look in the mirror to see where you should place your features. Can you make your picture look like you? Add ears, some sparkling teeth, and hair to look like yours.

Hand (and Foot) Art

Trace one of your hands on a sheet of paper. Instead of adding details like fingernails and knuckles, use your imagination! That hand tracing could be part of a bird's wing, or antlers on a deer. Look carefully: What do you see? Make a picture out of it.

ALIKE AND DIFFERENT

Look at other people. Does everyone have the same color eyes, the same shaped ears, nose, mouth, or the same length hair? People are alike because they have eyes, ears, nose, and mouth, but they are different, too.

MORE SURPRISES!

★ Trace the hands of different family members. Where do your hands fit in by size?

★ What are some things you can do with your hands? Here are a few things for you to try: **clap, pat, scratch, rub, tickle, lift, pull, push, wave, shake**, and **play pat-a-cake**. See if you can think of some others!

★ Your feet are pretty amazing, too! Try these with your feet: **wiggle, walk forwards, walk backwards, kick, run, jump, hop, tiptoe**, and **swing.**

I'm Thinking of Something

If we ask the right questions or are given the right clues, we can figure out what someone else is thinking without anyone even telling us.

 AGES 3-6

HERE'S WHAT YOU NEED

A partner

HERE'S WHAT YOU DO

1 Think of an object you can describe to your partner. For example, if you chose the word "apple," some clues to describe an apple are: round, red (or green or yellow), yummy, crunchy, good to eat, and grows on trees.

2 Start the game by giving your partner a clue: "I'm thinking of something that's round. Can you tell me what it is?" Your second clue might be: "I'm thinking of something that's round and red." Add clues one at a time, always letting your partner guess.

YUMMY CRUNCHY GOOD TO EAT GROWS ON TREES

ROUND

RED

MORE SURPRISES!

★ Choose an object in the room that you want your partner to guess. This time, instead of giving clues, your partner can ask questions that you can answer Yes or No, like "Is it red?"

★ Play "I Predict." Use your observation skills to predict what you are going to have for dinner, what the weather will be tomorrow, or if someone special is coming to visit.

Finger Food Fun

AGES 3-6

Here's one time when it is okay to play with your food!

HELPING · HANDS

Using multiple senses reinforces learning experiences. Finger Food Fun uses the senses of **sight, smell, touch**, and **taste** — a powerful combination of reinforcement. Children can play at their own level — from simple patterns to designs, shapes, letters, and numbers.

HERE'S WHAT YOU DO

1 Wash your hands and set out the finger foods on a clean table. Do you see any differences in the foods? Do raisins and carrot sticks look alike? Feel alike? Taste anything alike?

2 Make a shape with one food like pretzels; then make the same shape with a different food, like peanuts. Do you need the same number of pieces to make the same shape?

3 Ask a grown-up to write the first letter of your name in cereal. Then, you write the same letter in another food like carrot sticks. How do the letters look the same? Now, you can eat your letters! Do they taste the same or different?

MAKE A SQUARE WITH PRETZELS

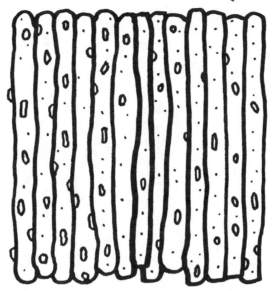

MAKE A SQUARE WITH PEANUTS

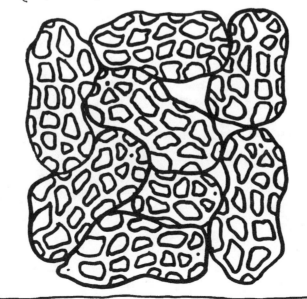

MORE SURPRISES!

★ Close your eyes and touch each food. Can you tell which is which just by **touching** them? Give yourself some hints by describing aloud what you are touching. Guess each food by **smelling** it and then by **tasting** it.

★ Choose one finger food, and use it to count. If you chose raisins, set down one raisin for the "One" pile. Then, set two raisins in a "Two" pile. Next would be the "Three" pile. See how many number piles you can make before you gobble them up.

Dice Designs

AGES 4-6

HERE'S WHAT YOU NEED

- 4-6 dice
- A partner

Comparing and copying dot designs on dice can be a fun way to learn and play.

Silly Thoughts!

Roll is a word that has a lot of different meanings: We roll dice to play a game, roll cookie dough with a rolling pin, teach a dog to roll over, and enjoy eating a warm roll fresh from the oven. How many times can you use the word roll in a silly story you make up?

HERE'S WHAT YOU DO

1 Roll one die. Count the number of dots that are showing. Set down another die so that the same number of dots are showing on top.

2 Roll two dice, and then place two more dice showing the same numbers. Take turns with a partner.

3 One partner places two or three dice in a pattern, and the other partner tries to create that same pattern.

4 For the Super Challenge, ask your partner to roll two dice. Take a close look at the dot design. Then ask your partner to cover the dice. Now, you try to set up your dice the same way.

HELPING·HANDS

Dice Designs provides experience in observation and reproducing patterns. This visual skill will be important in tasks like printing letters and numbers.

MORE SURPRISES!

★ Toss one die until it lands with only one dot on top. How many times did you have to toss it? Will it always take that many tosses to get one dot? Try it and see!

★ Close your eyes while a partner hides two dice in the room. Ask your partner to clap faster as you get closer to the hiding place.

★ Think of five things that are **bigger** than a die; then think of five things that are **smaller**!

Touch Will Tell

AGES 4-6

Your sense of touch can certainly tell you a lot. If you touch an ice cube, you learn that it is cold and hard; when you touch a kitten, you learn it is soft and fluffy.

HERE'S WHAT YOU DO

1. Ask a grown-up to draw a few letters (about 4") that you already know on the sandpaper. Cut out the letters and set aside.

2. Place the letters in a shoe box that has a hand-sized hole cut out of one end. Cover with the lid.

3. Reach into the hole and pick up any letter. Feel the letter's shape with your fingers. Try to picture it in your mind. Can you tell which letter you are holding just by feeling its shape?

Hint: Need some practice? Try holding the letter and feeling it while you are looking at it. Then, return it to the box and touch it again.

Safety First!

Things that are very sharp, like knives or grown-up scissors, can hurt you. Other things that are very hot, like the burners on a stove or very hot water, can hurt you, too. Can you think of any other things you shouldn't touch?

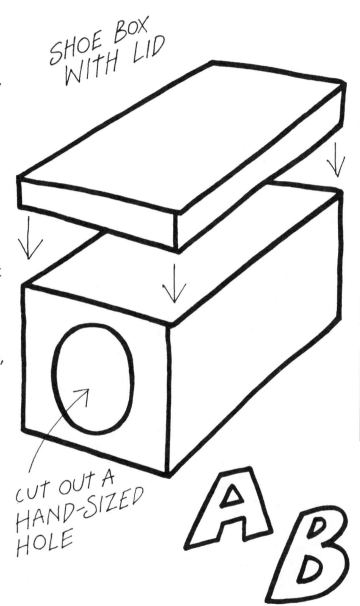

SHOE BOX WITH LID

CUT OUT A HAND-SIZED HOLE

MORE SURPRISES!

★ Close your eyes while a partner holds out from one to five fingers. Using touch only, count how many fingers are being held up. Now, count with your eyes open.

★ Instead of using sandpaper letters, try using sandpaper shapes or numbers.

★ Want a Super Challenge? Cut out your name in sandpaper letters. Close your eyes and arrange the letters to spell your name by touch.

A B C

CUT OUT SANDPAPER LETTERS

Three-Sense Challenge

AGES 4-6

Your senses of hearing, smelling, and touching can tell you where you are — and a whole lot more!

MORE SURPRISES!

HERE'S WHAT YOU NEED

A blindfold (handkerchief)

A grown-up partner

HERE'S WHAT YOU DO

1 Ask a grown-up to cover your eyes loosely with a handkerchief blindfold. (Or, you can just keep your eyes closed tightly.)

2 The grown-up will hold one of your hands and walk you slowly to another room. Can you guess where you are by using your senses of hearing, smelling, and touching?

HELPING•HANDS

Start out simply, and ask questions that will help. If a child says, "I can smell bacon," you could respond, "Where do we cook bacon?"

★ Would you hear these sounds indoors or outdoors: a clock ticking, a horn honking, birds chirping, water running in a sink, food sizzling?

★ Would you smell these scents indoors or outdoors: dinner cooking, a man's aftershave, burning leaves, pine trees?

★ Try eating a snack without peeking, or try getting dressed without opening your eyes! What sense did you get clues from?

I Understand!

The hungry dinosaur ate a snack.

I was hungry and ate a snack of dinosaur crackers.

These two sentences use a lot of the same words, but they have very different meanings, don't they? Language helps us to share our thoughts and to learn about what other people think.

Animals In Our House!

Paper lunch bag

Magazines

Scissors and glue

Slips of paper

Don't look now, but I think there's an elephant in your house!

AGES 2-6

HERE'S WHAT YOU DO

1 Look through old magazines for pictures of animals. Cut them out and glue them on slips of paper. Fold and place in the paper bag.

2 Pull a slip of paper from the bag. What animal did you pick? Think about your animal — how it moves, how it rests, what it eats, and what sound it makes. Picture your animal in your mind and pretend that you are that animal!

Silly Sayings

That's more fun than a barrel of monkeys!

It's easy to understand how monkeys can be fun to watch, but can you imagine monkeys in a barrel? Maybe you can make up your own silly animal sayings. How about this one: That's more fun than pigs in a mud puddle!

MORE SURPRISES!

★ Pretend that you're filling a zoo with animals. Before you can add an animal, you have to be able to imitate it. Now, fill your zoo with lots of animals.

★ Instead of animals, act out different types of weather. Can you pretend to be a thunderstorm? A falling snowflake? Hail? A raindrop? A tornado? Sunshine?

HELPING · HANDS

Compare animals with each other. For example, the monkey is small and moves quickly and playfully, while the elephant is large and moves slowly while swinging its trunk. Words like **slowly** and **quickly** have clearer meaning when a child acts them out.

Rhymes and Finger Plays

Tell a story or make someone giggle with rhymes and hand motions.

AGES 2-6

FIVE LITTLE MONKEYS JUMPING ON THE BED

HELPING·HANDS

Finger plays are a fun way to enjoy language together. To help a young child learn finger plays, have the child sit on your lap so you can move your hands together.

HERE'S WHAT YOU DO

1 Sit across from your partner as you say the rhyme together, making hand motions together.

Five Little Monkeys

Five little monkeys (hold up five fingers)
Jumping on the bed (one fist "bounces" on the palm of the other hand)

One fell off and bumped his head (hands bump together)
Mama called the doctor and the doctor said (pretend to hold the phone to your ear)

"No more monkeys jumping on the bed!" (wiggle your pointing finger)

Repeat verse and hand motions for four, three, two, and one little monkey.

★ As you learn to count higher and higher, maybe you'll want to change Five Little Monkeys to Ten Little Monkeys, and then to twenty.

★ Make up some finger plays to your favorite rhymes, poems, and songs like *She'll Be Coming 'Round the Mountain, Eensy, Weensy Spider,* and *Baa, Baa Black Sheep.*

★ *Wee Sing Silly Songs* is a cassette and book of silly songs and rhymes. Read and listen to songs and clap out rhythms.

I Like...

AGES 3-6

Create a book that's all about things you like and dislike — and it will be one-of-a-kind, just like you!

HERE'S WHAT YOU NEED

- Old magazines
- Construction paper
- Safety scissors
- Paste
- Paper punch
- Crayon or marker
- Yarn

HERE'S WHAT YOU DO

1 Cut out magazine pictures of things you like . . . and things you don't like, too. Put them in two separate piles.

2 With a grown-up's help, print "I like" or "I don't like" at the top of some pages of construction paper. Paste the pictures on the appropriate pieces of paper.

3 Make a cover for your book from a sheet of construction paper. Give your book a title and draw a special picture of yourself on the cover.

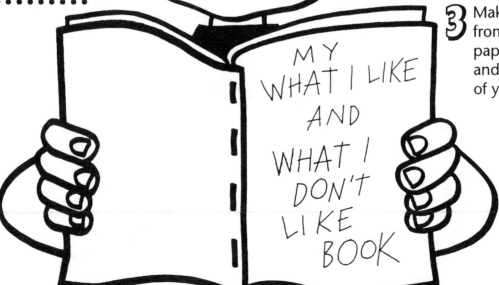

MY WHAT I LIKE AND WHAT I DON'T LIKE BOOK

"All About Me" Collage

If you like to cut and paste, create a collage all about you. Cut and glue pictures about you and your interests onto a large sheet of paper.

★ Practice reading your book often. Remember to read the words "I like" or "I don't like" at the top of each page. Ask your friends what they like or don't like so you can learn more about them, too!

★ As you think of other things you like, add pages to your book. If you can't find the pictures in magazines, you can draw them yourself.

HELPING • HANDS
Besides its great motivational value, the simple word pattern in the book makes it one that a child can easily "read."

Tricky Tales

It's fun to listen to your favorite stories over and over. But, what if someone changed some of the words? Listen for the "trick" words.

AGES 3-6

ONCE UPON A TIME

HERE'S WHAT YOU NEED

Some of your favorite books

A grown-up partner

HERE'S WHAT YOU DO

1 Ask your grown-up partner to read one of your favorite stories aloud, changing some of the more familiar words.

2 Listen very carefully! Every time you hear a word that doesn't belong, shout "STOP!" Can you tell your partner what the real word is?

ALIKE AND DIFFERENT

"Little Red Riding Hood" and "Goldilocks and the Three Bears" are alike because both begin with young girls who go walking through the woods. One way they are different is that Little Red Riding Hood went to visit her grandmother, while Goldilocks visited the bears' house. What else is alike and different about these two stories?

GOLDILOCKS

LITTLE RED RIDING HOOD

MORE SURPRISES!

★ Make some finger puppets and act out your favorite story as a grown-up reads it aloud. Invite a friend to act it out with you.

★ When you hear the words, "Once upon a time....," do you know what's going to happen? That's right: a story is about to begin! Make up your own "Once upon a time" story to share with your friends.

HELPING · HANDS

Choose familiar stories to read aloud. As you slowly read through the stories, make obvious and silly changes, like "Goldilocks carried the shoelace full of food to Grandmother's house." To switch roles with older children, they can tell the story, substituting funny words for a grown-up or friend to catch.

Noise Makers

HERE'S WHAT YOU NEED

- Handful of dried beans
- Paper plates
- Crayons
- Stapler and tape
- Popsicle stick

What's one word that always gets your attention? Your name! Here's an activity just for you that's all about listening for a special word.

Lip Reading

Ask a partner to choose an object somewhere in the room without telling you what it is. Then, cover both your ears, and look at your partner's mouth while the word is whispered. Can you tell the word by lip reading?

HERE'S WHAT YOU DO

1 Draw a picture on the back of two paper plates.

2 Flip one plate over so it's right-side up. Tape a Popsicle stick to the plate leaving out part of the stick for a handle.

3 To make a noisemaker, pour the dried beans in the center of this plate. Staple the plates together face-to-face so the beans won't fall out.

4 Choose one of your favorite stories and pick a name or rhyme that is repeated in the story often. As the story is read aloud, shake your noisemaker every time you hear your word or rhyme.

HELPING·HANDS

Read the story a little more slowly than usual, providing a better opportunity to focus on individual words.

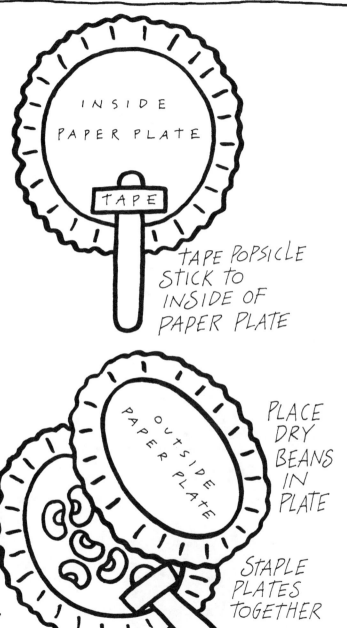

INSIDE PAPER PLATE

TAPE

TAPE POPSICLE STICK TO INSIDE OF PAPER PLATE

OUTSIDE PAPER PLATE

PLACE DRY BEANS IN PLATE

STAPLE PLATES TOGETHER

MORE SURPRISES!

★ Take turns reciting some nursery rhymes or favorite songs. Pick an important word and shake your noisemaker every time you say that word.

★ Pick a key word from another story. This time, close your eyes as you listen to the story. Is it easier or more difficult to listen closely with your eyes closed?

★ Here's another noise-maker to make. Decorate a paper lunch bag, pour in some dried beans, blow some air into the bag, and tie tightly around the opening with yarn.

Five-Finger Hunt

AGES 4-6

Five is a special number. It's the number of fingers you have on each hand, and the number of toes you have on each foot!

ONE
TWO
THREE
FOUR
FIVE

HERE'S WHAT YOU DO

1 Five is how many things you can hunt for in this game. Let's find five things that are red.

2 With your partner, walk around and look for red things. Each time you find one, count and touch a different finger on your hand, starting with your thumb. That way, you'll know when you get to five.

3 Now that you know how to play Five Finger Hunt, choose another category of fun things to hunt for. Here are some ideas to get you started: five things that are cold, five things that are big, five things that are little, five things that are heavy, or five things that are blue. Happy hunting!

HELPING • HANDS

Five Finger Hunt helps children to categorize and apply descriptive words (big, round, red) to different objects. You can easily modify this to fit each child's abilities and personality. Choose categories that each child is familiar with, moving from colors to sizes to shapes to objects beginning with a particular letter sound.

MORE SURPRISES!

★ How would you like to find five things that are round, or five that are square? Find a ball to carry with you so you know what something round looks like; a block will remind you of a square.

★ Play Five Finger Hunt outdoors. Here are some outdoor hunt ideas: five things that are green, five things that smell good, five things that have wings, five things that are four-legged, five things that bark, five things that are smaller than your foot, five things that live in a tree.

Happy-Sad Masks

 AGES 4-6

HERE'S WHAT YOU NEED

- 2 paper plates
- 2 Popsicle sticks
- Crayons
- Tape or glue
- A favorite storybook

*There are lots of ways to feel, and
all of them are a part of who we are.*

HERE'S WHAT YOU DO

1 Look in a mirror and make a happy face. On one of the paper plates, draw a happy face just like yours.

2 How is a sad face different from a happy face? One difference is that instead of a happy smile, the mouth turns downward in a frown. Draw a sad face on the second paper plate.

3 On the back of each plate, tape or glue a Popsicle stick to make a handle.

4 Ask a grown-up to read you a story. Listen very carefully. When the story is sad, hold up your sad mask. When the story is happy, hold up the happy mask.

ALIKE AND DIFFERENT

Place your two masks side by side. How are the two masks alike? Here's one way: Each mask has two eyes. Can you think of other ways the two masks are alike? Now, how are they different?

SURPRISED

ANGRY

MORE SURPRISES!

★ Look in a mirror to see how you look when you are happy, sad, or angry.

★ Make up a play to perform for your friends using your new masks to show when the characters are sad or happy.

★ Make a few more masks to express other feelings, like a surprised mask or an angry mask.

HELPING·HANDS

Happy-Sad Masks help children connect words with feelings and actions. Choose familiar stories so children can focus on words that express feelings.

Recycled Greeting Cards

HERE'S WHAT YOU NEED

- Old greeting cards
- Crayons
- Pencil
- Construction paper
- Safety scissors
- Glue

AGES 4-6

Make a special card out of an old greeting card. You'll have fun making it and making someone happy with it, too.

HERE'S WHAT YOU DO

1 To make your card very special, think about who the card is for and what you want it to say.

2 Look through old greeting cards and cut out any pictures you think that person would like. Fold a piece of construction paper in half. Lay the pictures on it and glue them into place. Save a spot where you can use your crayons to draw a special picture of your own.

3 Ask a grown-up to print out your message in pencil, then you trace over it in crayon. Print your name and send some hugs (O's) and kisses (X's), too.

HELPING · HANDS

Recycled Greeting Cards encourages children to express themselves on paper with both words and art. Anytime is the right time for this activity.

Movin' & Shakin'

Do you like to wiggle your fingers and crinkle your toes? What about run, jump, hop, and bounce? Movin' and shakin' - whether playing Hide and Seek or cutting paper with scissors — are lots of fun!

Paper Burst

 AGES 2-4

When people run in a race, the first runner bursts through the ribbon to cross the finish line. You can be the winner!

HERE'S WHAT YOU NEED

A newspaper

2 partners

HERE'S WHAT YOU DO

1. Ask your partners to each hold one side of a sheet of newspaper. Move far back from them, giving yourself a lot of room to run before you reach the newspaper/finish line.

2. Now it's time to "turn on" your wonderful imagination and run the race! Close your eyes for a moment and pretend you are the fastest runner in the world, lined up at the starting line. On your mark, get set, GO!

3. Turn on your best burst of speed to win the race, as you tear through the paper. Take turns with your partners being the runner.

HELPING·HANDS

Paper Burst is a fun way to combine gross motor practice with imagination and visualization.

MORE SURPRISES!

★ Use your imagination to run the race, each time as a different animal. Pretend that you're a dog running a race — only this time, you'll be running on your hands and feet. Here are some other animals to run as:

bird — flapping wings

ant — tiny, tiny steps

kangaroo — jumping steps

monkey — swinging from tree to tree

★ Go to a race — bike, running, swimming — and be part of the crowd cheering on the athletes.

Paint With Water

 AGES 2-6

HERE'S WHAT YOU NEED

Plastic bowl

Assorted paintbrushes

Bathing suit

Water

Combining painting and playing with water makes for twice the fun!

HERE'S WHAT YOU DO

1 After you've put on your bathing suit, bring a bowl filled half-way with water and some paintbrushes outdoors.

2 Pick something to "water paint" — the ground, cement, a leaf, a stick, a rock — and watch what happens when you brush it with water. Does the water sit on top, or does it soak in and disappear? Does it dry quickly or slowly?

3 Paint different objects using both large and small brushes. Then, paint a big picture on the ground using water.

HELPING • HANDS

Water Painting involves fine motor skills (using paintbrushes), gross motor skills (painting large areas), observation skills, and verbal skills as children talk about their paintings.

SILLY SAYINGS

A picture is worth a thousand words.

Do you have a favorite picture book that tells a story without using words?

MORE SURPRISES!

★ As you sing one of your favorite songs, paint a water design about your song on the ground or cement. Let the melody, rhythm, and words inspire you!

★ Choose two things to paint with water. After you've painted both, watch and see which dries the fastest. Why do you think that happened?

★ Although water doesn't have a color, it can change the color of other things. Do any of the things you painted become darker or lighter when they get wet, or do they stay the same?

Obstacle Course

AGES 3-6

Move your body in all sorts of ways, while meeting different challenges along the way.

HERE'S WHAT YOU NEED

A beanbag or washcloth

Chair

Open, clear play area

HERE'S WHAT YOU DO

1. Set up an obstacle course with a start and finish line and several obstacles. Here's an example of an obstacle course: Run to the chair, sit down, roll on the ground to the beanbag, pick it up, and crawl to the finish line.

2. For added fun, ask a grown-up to time you and then see if you can beat your own time with practice.

HELPING•HANDS

Provide a safe course that encourages good motor skill development and mental flexibility, as well as directional concept development.

MORE SURPRISES!

★ Create a special **Over** and **Under** Obstacle Course, such as scrambling over the seat of the chair first, then crawling under it on the way back.

★ Set up an **Around** and **Between** Obstacle Course with two chairs, walking around them the first time, and hopping between them on the way back.

★ Ask a grown-up to draw some mazes — an obstacle course on paper — for you to solve.

Bounce and Count

AGES 3-6

Bounce it, roll it, throw it, toss it, catch it — and now, count it, too!

HERE'S WHAT YOU DO

1 Sit on the ground about 10 feet away from your partner. Practice rolling the ball back and forth.

2 Say "One!" in a nice, loud voice, and roll the ball to your partner. Your partner must say "Two!" before rolling it back to you. You say "Three!," and send the ball back. Keep rolling the ball back and forth until you can't count any higher.

3 Next game, toss the ball, letting it bounce before your partner catches it. Before you throw it, call out a number. When your partner catches the ball, he or she must say the next number. Count each time the ball is tossed and each time it is caught.

MORE SURPRISES!

★ Call out a number between one and five; that's how many times the ball is rolled back and forth.

★ How many times can you dribble a ball in a row without missing it? Count the number of dribbles out loud.

HELPING·HANDS Focus on numbers lower than ten. Take turns starting on the number one so each child is exposed to different numbers.

Build-A-Person

AGES 3-6

Eyes, noses, mouths, feet, arms, hands, and legs. Build-A-Person the way you think these should all go together.

HELPING · HANDS

Build-A-Person provides a good opportunity to encourage creative thinking and to avoid physical stereotypes.

HERE'S WHAT YOU DO

1. Look through some magazines for pictures of people. Instead of cutting out the whole person, cut out a hand from one picture, a foot from another, an eye, mouth, ear from others, and so on.

2. Ask a grown-up to draw the outline of a person on a piece of paper. Then, take turns picking a cutout and placing it on the outline until you have built a person. How does it look?

3. Compare your person with a picture in a magazine. Do you have the same number of eyes? Ears? Hands and feet? If you want, rearrange some features on your person; then, glue your person together, drawing in anything missing.

CUT OUT AND GLUE ON PICTURES OF MOUTHS, EYES, EARS

CUT OUT AND GLUE ON PICTURES OF HANDS

CUT OUT AND GLUE ON PICTURES OF FEET

↑ OUTLINE ON PAPER

MORE SURPRISES!

★ Other things to build with cutouts: a car, an airplane, a dog, a house.

ALIKE AND DIFFERENT

Something that's really wonderful about people is that none of us are exactly alike. Even though we share a lot of the same features, there are so many ways we are different. Can you think of a few?

Cutting Up! ★

AGES 3-6

HERE'S WHAT YOU NEED

- Safety scissors
- Play dough
- Construction paper cut into one-inch strips
- Place mat

Scissors are very helpful tools with many, many uses. Have fun here cutting with safety scissors.

HERE'S WHAT YOU DO

1. Put your fingers in the scissor holes. Open, close, open, close. Place the play dough in a large lump on the place mat. Cut the play dough into different-sized pieces like large chunks, or tiny strips like spaghetti.

2. Now, cut a strip of paper. Can you cut it in half with one open-close snip? Cut lots of paper strips.

3. Draw a long straight line down a sheet of paper. Try following the line as you cut with your scissors. Next, make a curved line that you can cut along.

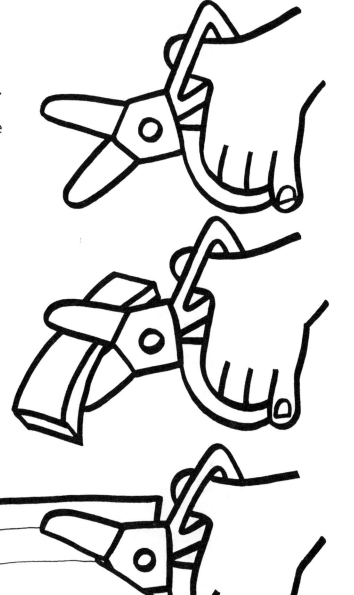

★ Make confetti by cutting lots of little pieces from your paper scraps. Save the pieces and use them in a special celebration.

★ Cut paper strips from different-colored construction paper or recycled gift wrap. Then make a paper chain to hang around your room.

HELPING·HANDS

Two helpful scissors rules: "Thumbs up!" means to keep the side of the scissors with your thumb in it facing up. "Turn the paper, not the scissors!" If you turn the scissors, you'll turn your arm, and that's not as comfortable as just turning the paper.

Opposites Attract

AGES 3-6

Opposites are two things that are as different from each other as they can get.

HERE'S WHAT YOU NEED

A partner

HERE'S WHAT YOU DO

1. Do the opposite of whatever your partner does. Stand facing each other. Watch carefully. If your partner stands up, you sit down. If your partner smiles, you frown. Here are some more opposite actions you can do with your partner:

smile >>>>>>>>>> frown

reach up >>>>>>> reach down

hop on one foot > stand still

laugh >>>>>>>>>> pretend to cry

squat down >>>>> jump high

whisper >>>>>>>> shout

ALIKE AND DIFFERENT

Like two peas in a pod.
As different as night and day.

Some of these sayings mean things that are opposites, and some mean things that are the same. Can you figure out which are which?

MORE SURPRISES!

★ Play opposite words. For every word your partner says, you say the opposite. Here are some to get you started: hot, rainy, black, new, big, hello, tall, in, on, come, high. Take turns giving the word.

★ For a Super Challenge, don't say the word; instead, act it out. Your partner has to act out the opposite.

Yes, I Can! ★

Here's a chance to do some grown-up things and discover all that you can do.

HERE'S WHAT YOU NEED

A grown-up partner

HERE'S WHAT YOU DO

1. Choose an around-the-house activity to do with grown-up supervision. Before you begin, be sure you have the necessary tools. Ask someone to show you how, and then do it yourself!

- crack an egg
- separate egg yolks from egg whites
- mix batter with a spoon
- sort laundry
- scour a pot
- tie a knot
- fold clothes
- put clothes away
- dust
- tighten loose screws
- replace a roll of toilet tissue
- make your bed
- ice cupcakes with a spatula
- roll out dough with a rolling pin
- thread a shoe with a shoelace

2. After you finish an activity, help with the clean-up and start thinking about what you'd like to try next. Isn't it fun helping at home?

★ Try these activities first with one hand, then with the other: mix with a spoon, scour a pot, dust, tighten a loose screw, sort laundry, ice cupcakes.

★ Invite a friend over. With grown-up supervision, teach your friend how to do one of the projects you just learned to do. How do you like being a teacher?

When I Grow Up

Do you know what you'd like to do when you grow up? Pretend that you're a grown-up and you're on your way to work. Dress up in your work clothes, and act out what you think you would do at your place of work.

Two Hands — Or One!

HERE'S WHAT YOU NEED

Toy blocks

Paper

Pencil or crayon

AGES 4-6

Sometimes we use one hand, but sometimes two hands work better!

HERE'S WHAT YOU DO

1 Using only one hand, see how high you can stack building blocks before the stack falls over. Count how many blocks were in that stack. Then, try the same thing using your other hand. Now, stack the blocks using both hands. Which stack was highest?

2 Draw a curved line and a wavy line on one sheet of paper, and a circle, square, and triangle on another. Trace over them with one finger. Now, switch hands and try again. Can you do this with two hands together? Which hand were you more comfortable tracing with?

3 Next, color in two shapes with one hand, and two shapes with the other. Are you beginning to find using one hand is more comfortable than using the other, or are both hands the same?

Two-Handed Puppets

With a little imagination, your hands can be puppets. On each hand, your thumb is the lower lip, and your pointing finger is the upper lip. Practice opening and closing the "mouth" of your pretend puppets.

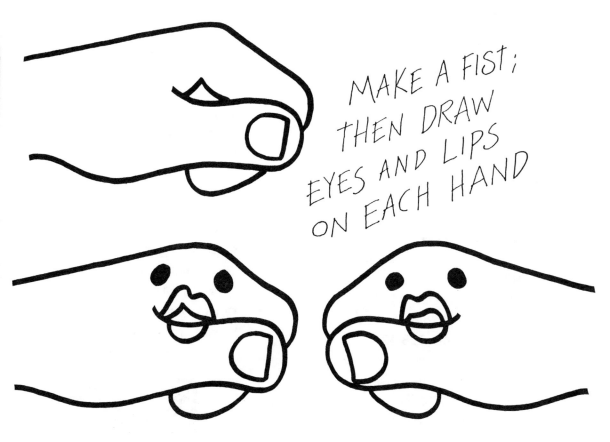

MAKE A FIST; THEN DRAW EYES AND LIPS ON EACH HAND

★ Try stacking coins with one hand, then the other. Then try making a stack of coins using both hands.

★ Throw a ball, first using one hand and then the other. Which hand is it easier to throw with? What about kicking a ball?

★ Catch a ball. Can you catch with one hand or is it easier to catch with two hands?

HELPING · HANDS

Most children will eventually express a preference for right-handed-ness or left-handedness. Allow each child to follow his or her natural preference.

Index to Early Learning Skills

color recognition, 23-34
   Coffee Can Color Sort, 28-29
   Color Walk, 30-31
   Five Finger Hunt, 114-115
   Ice Painting, 34
   Racing Colors, 32-33
   Shaving Cream Pictures, 26-27
   Tissue Paper Rainbow, 24-25
   Travel Hunt, 18-19

compare/contrast, 81-102
   Animal Round-Up!, 74-75
   Animals In Our House!, 104-105
   Big and Little Day, 86-87
   Big and Small, 68-69
   Build-A-Person, 128-129
   Coffee Can Color Sort, 28-29
   Counting Pictograph, 64-66
   Dice Designs, 98-99
   Dough Bead Necklace, 78-79
   Face Fun, 52-53
   Finger Food Fun, 96-97

   Happy-Sad Masks, 116-117
   I Like..., 108-109
   I'm Thinking of Something, 94-95
   In The Bag, 88-89
   Make-A-Match, 46-47
   Matching Groups, 80
   Memories Box, 76-77
   Mirror Pals, 84-85
   Noise Makers, 112-113
   Obstacle Course, 124-125
   Opposites Attract, 132-133
   Recycled Greeting Cards, 118
   Self-Portraits, 92-93
   Three-Sense Challenge, 102
   Touch Will Tell, 100-101
   What's Missing?, 90-91
   What's That Sound?, 82-83

comprehension, 103-118
Animals In Our House!, 104-105
Build-A-Person, 128-129
Five Finger Hunt, 114-115
Happy-Sad Masks, 116-117
I Like..., 108-109
Noise Makers, 112-113
Paint With Water, 122-123
Recycled Greeting Cards, 118
Rhymes and Finger Plays, 106-107
Tricky Tales, 110-111

counting, 49-66
Animal Round-Up!, 74-75
Bounce and Count, 126-127
Count-and-Eat Jewelry, 54-55
Counting Pictograph, 64-66
Creative Creatures, 62-63
Dice Designs, 98-99
Egg Carton Count, 50-51
Face Fun, 52-53
Finger Food Fun, 96-97

Five Finger Hunt, 114-115
Jumping Numbers, 56-57
Number Puzzles, 58-59
Paper Chain Counting Calendar, 60-61
Rhymes and Finger Plays, 106-107
Touch Will Tell, 100-101
Two Hands — Or One!, 136-137
see also number recognition

fine motor skills
Build-A-Person, 128-129
Count-and-Eat Jewelry, 54-55
Creative Creatures, 62-63
Cutting Up!, 130-131
Dough Bead Necklace, 78-79
Egg Carton Count, 50-51
Paint With Water, 122-123
Paper Chain Counting Calendar, 60-61
Pudding Paint Designs, 12-13
Self-Portraits, 92-93
Shaving Cream Pictures, 26-27
Yes, I Can!, 134-135

gross motor skills, 119-137
Body Letters, 42-43
Bounce and Count, 126-127
Jumping Numbers, 56-57
Mirror Pals, 84-85
Obstacle Course, 124-125
Opposites Attract, 132-133
Paint With Water, 122-123
Paper Burst, 120-121
Rhymes and Finger Plays, 106-107
Self-Portraits, 92-93
Two Hands — Or One!, 136-137
Yes, I Can!, 134-135

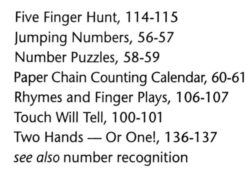

letter recognition, 35-48
ABC Cookies, 36-37
Bean Fun, 40-41
Body Letters, 42-43
Make-A-Match, 46-47
Palm Drawings, 44-45
Trace-A-Letter, 38-39

listening
Happy-Sad Masks, 116-117
Noise Makers, 112-113
Three-Sense Challenge, 102
Tricky Tales, 110-111
What's That Sound?, 82-83

memory skill builders
Body Letters, 42-43
In The Bag, 88-89
Make-A-Match, 46-48
What's Missing?, 90-91

number recognition, 49-66
Count-and-Eat Jewelry, 54-55
Counting Pictograph, 64-66
Creative Creatures, 62-63
Egg Carton Count, 50-51
Face Fun, 52-53
Jumping Numbers, 56-57
Number Puzzles, 58-59
Paper Chain Counting Calendar, 60-61

observation
Color Walk, 30-31
Dice Designs, 98-99
Face Fun, 52-53
I'm Thinking of Something, 94-95
Paint With Water, 122-123
Self-Portraits, 92-93
Shape Detective, 20-21
What's Missing?, 90-91

sensory awareness
Bean Fun, 40-41
Coffee Can Color Sort, 28-29
Finger Food Fun, 96-97
Imagination Station, 72-73
In The Bag, 88-89
Number Puzzles, 58-59
Palm Drawings, 44-45
Pudding Paint Designs, 12-13
Shape Art, 8-9
Three-Sense Challenge, 102
Touch Will Tell, 100-101

shape recognition, 7-22

    Bean Fun, 40-41

    Book of Shapes, 10-11

    Coffee Can Color Sort, 28-29

    Finger Food Fun, 96-97

    Five Finger Hunt, 114-115

    Place Mat Patterns, 14-15

    Plenty of Patterns, 22

    Pudding Paint Designs, 12-13

    Shape Art, 8-9

    Shape Detective, 20-21

    Shaving Cream Pictures, 26-27

    Sponge Paint Shapes, 16-17

    Trace-A-Letter, 38-39

    Travel Hunt, 18-19

    Two Hands — Or One!, 136-137

sorting, 67-80

    Animal Round-Up, 74-75

    Bean Fun, 40-41

    Big and Little Day, 86-87

    Big and Small, 68-69

    Coffee Can Color Sort, 28-29

    Color Walk, 30-31

    Dough Bead Necklace, 78-79

    Five Finger Hunt, 114-115

    Food Sort, 70-71

    I Like..., 108-109

    Imagination Station, 72-73

    Make-A-Match, 46-48

    Matching Groups, 80

    Memories Box, 76-77

    Place Mat Patterns, 14-15

    Plenty of Patterns, 22

    Travel Hunt, 18-19

The following *Kids Can!* books for ages 4 to 10 are each 160-178 pages, fully illustrated, trade paper, 11 x 8 1/2, $12.95 US. Please see last page for ordering information.

SUPER SCIENCE CONCOCTIONS
50 Mysterious Mixtures for Fabulous Fun
by Jill Frankel Hauser

THE KIDS' MULTICULTURAL COOKBOOK
Food & Fun Around the World
by Deanna F. Cook

Children's Book-of-the-Month Selection!
KIDS' COMPUTER CREATIONS
Using Your Computer for Art & Craft Fun
by Carol Sabbeth

KIDS GARDEN!
The Anytime, Anyplace Guide to Sowing & Growing Fun
by Avery Hart and Paul Mantell

Winner of the Oppenheim Toy Portfolio Best Book Award!
American Bookseller Pick of the Lists
THE KIDS' SCIENCE BOOK
Creative Experiences for Hands-On Fun
by Robert Hirschfeld and Nancy White

Parents' Choice Gold Award Winner!
American Bookseller Pick of the Lists
THE KIDS' MULTICULTURAL ART BOOK
Art & Craft Experiences from Around the World
by Alexandra M. Terzian

Parents' Choice Gold Award Winner!
Benjamin Franklin Best Juvenile Nonfiction Award Winner!
KIDS MAKE MUSIC!
Clapping and Tapping from Bach to Rock
by Avery Hart and Paul Mantell

Children's Book-of-the-Month Main Selection!
KIDS & WEEKENDS!
Creative Ways to Make Special Days
by Avery Hart and Paul Mantell

American Bookseller Pick of the Lists
KIDS' CRAZY CONCOCTIONS
50 Mysterious Mixtures for Art & Craft Fun
by Jill Frankel Hauser

Winner of the Oppenheim Toy Portfolio Best Book Award!
Skipping Stones Nature & Ecology Honor Award Winner!
EcoArt!
Earth-Friendly Art & Craft Experiences for 3- to 9-Year-Olds
by Laurie Carlson

A Better Homes & Gardens Book Club Selection!
KIDS COOK!
Fabulous Food for the Whole Family
by Sarah Williamson and Zachary Williamson

THE KIDS' WILDLIFE BOOK
Exploring Animal Worlds through Indoor/Outdoor Crafts & Experiences
by Warner Shedd

HANDS AROUND THE WORLD
365 Creative Ways to Build Cultural Awareness & Global Respect
by Susan Milord

Parents' Choice Gold Award Winner!
Parents Magazine Parents' Pick!
THE KIDS' NATURE BOOK
365 Indoor/Outdoor Activities and Experiences
by Susan Milord

KIDS CREATE!
Art & Craft Experiences for 3- to 9-Year-Olds
by Laurie Carlson

Parents Magazine Parents' Pick!
KIDS LEARN AMERICA!
Bringing Geography to Life with People, Places, & History
by Patricia Gordon and Reed C. Snow

American Bookseller Pick of the Lists
ADVENTURES IN ART
Art & Craft Experiences for 7- to 14-Year-Olds
by Susan Milord

WILLIAMSON  *LITTLE HANDS* BOOKS

The following *Little Hands* books for ages 2 to 6 are each 144 pages, fully illustrated, trade paper, 10 x 8, $12.95 US.

STOP, LOOK, & LISTEN!
Exploring Your Senses from Head to Toe
by Sarah A. Williamson

SUNNY DAYS & STARRY NIGHTS
A Little Hands Nature Book
by Nancy Fusco Castaldo

RAINY DAY PLAY!
Explore, Create, Discover, Pretend
by Nancy Fusco Castaldo

Children's Book-of-the-Month Main Selection
THE LITTLE HANDS ART BOOK
Exploring Arts & Crafts with 2- to 6-Year-Olds
by Judy Press

The Little Hands
BIG FUN CRAFT BOOK
Creative Fun for 2- to 6-Year-Olds
by Judy Press

Little Hands is a registered trademark of Williamson Publishing.

To Order:

Ask for WILLIAMSON books at your favorite bookstore. Or, order directly from WILLIAMSON PUBLISHING. We accept Visa and MasterCard (please include the number and expiration date), or send check to:

Williamson Publishing Company
Church Hill Road, P.O. Box 185
Charlotte, Vermont 05445

Toll-free phone orders with credit cards:
1-800-234-8791

Please add $3.00 for postage for one book plus 50 cents for each additional book. Satisfaction is guaranteed or full refund without questions or quibbles.

Prices may be slightly higher when purchased in Canada.